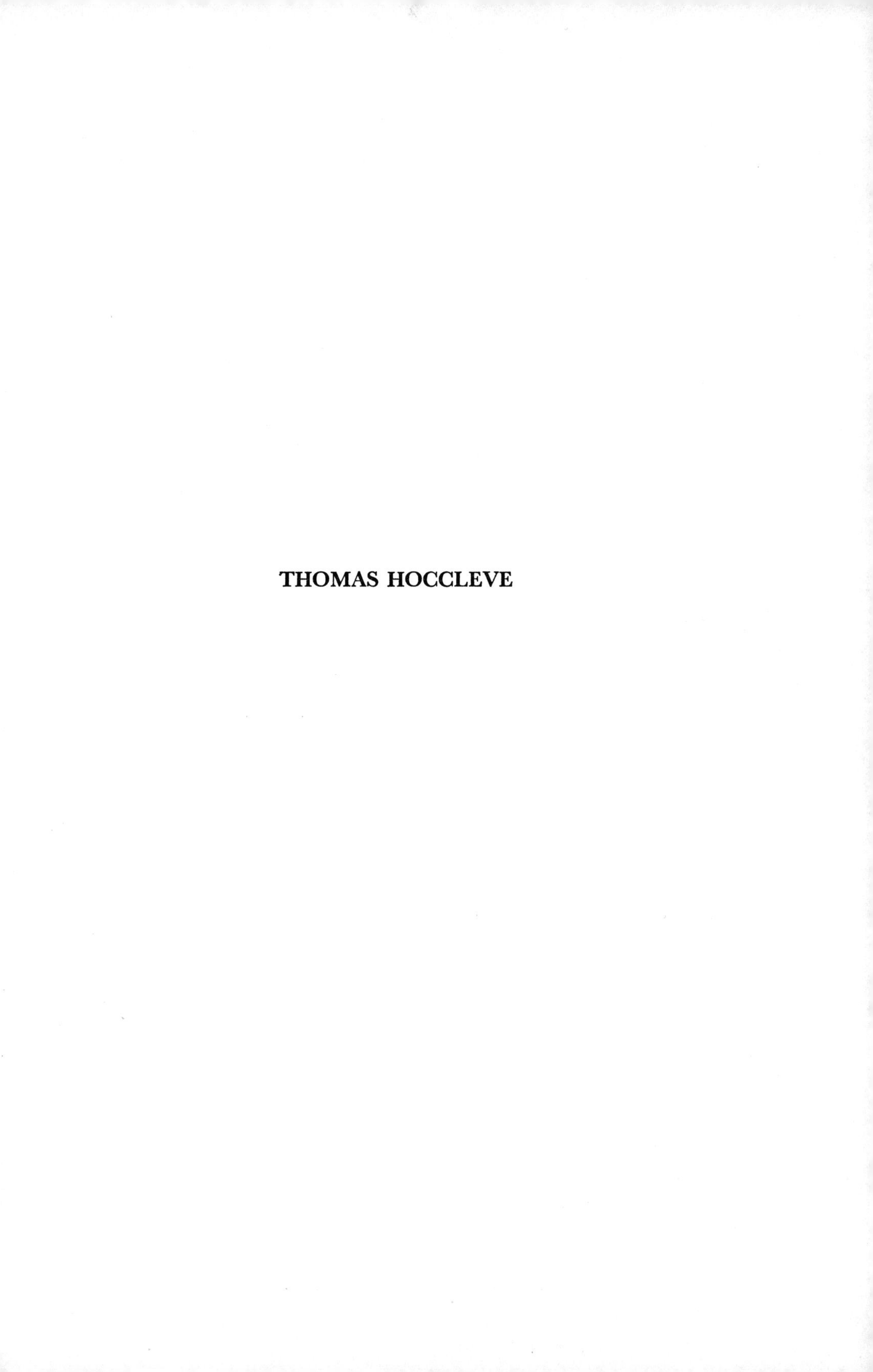

THOMAS HOCCLEVE

Frontispiece: Hoccleve presenting a copy of the *Regement of Princes* to Prince Henry (from Brit. Mus. MS. Royal 17. D. vi).

Hye and noble prince excellent
My lord the prince my lord gratious
I humble seruaunt and obedient
Vnto your estate hye and glorious
Of which I am full tendir and full ielous
Me recommaunde vnto your worthynesse
With hert entier and spirite of mekenesse

JEROME MITCHELL

THOMAS HOCCLEVE

A Study in Early Fifteenth-Century English Poetic

UNIVERSITY OF ILLINOIS PRESS
URBANA · CHICAGO · LONDON, 1968

Manufactured in the United States of America
Library of Congress Catalog Card No. 67-21855

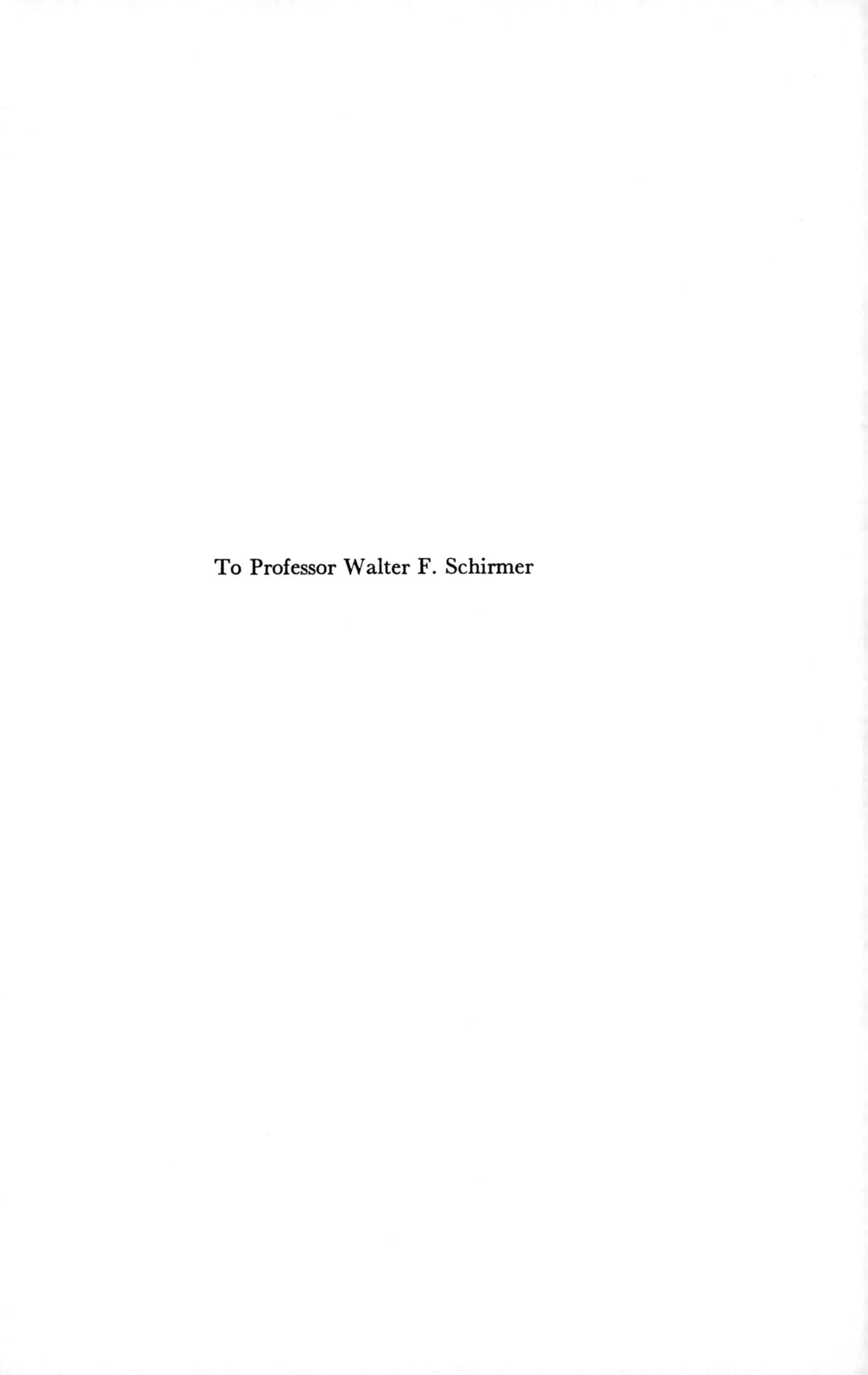

To Professor Walter F. Schirmer

PREFACE

The appendix to the present study consists of an annotated Hoccleve bibliography, which brings together all previous Hoccleve scholarship and establishes a complete overview. The state of Hoccleve scholarship can be summarized in a few words. To begin with, the canon has long been established. Frederick J. Furnivall introduced a difficulty when he suggested that the poems in Brit. Mus. MS. Egerton 615 were by Hoccleve (see my bibliography, item II.A.4), but Henry Noble MacCracken (III.18) and J. H. Kern (III.11) have shown that he was mistaken. Second, all Hoccleve's poems have been edited, some of them more than once. The first important printed texts were prepared by George Mason (II.A.1), Thomas Wright (II.B.13), and Lucy Toulmin Smith (II.B.2). The definitive and only complete edition is the work of Furnivall (II.A.2 & 4) and Sir Israel Gollancz (II.A.3). Many of Furnivall's editorial mistakes have been pointed out by Kern (III.13). Important twentieth-century editions of separate poems have been done by Eleanor Prescott Hammond (II.C.5), Rossell Hope Robbins (II.B.3 & 14), and Beverly Boyd (II.B.9). Several nontextual studies have contributed much to a better understanding of Hoccleve's verse. The most outstanding of these are source studies by Friedrich Aster (III.1) and Benjamin P. Kurtz (III.15); biographical studies by Furnivall (II.A.2), Kern (III.11), and H. S. Bennett (III.2); and an article on the Hoccleve autograph manuscripts by H. C. Schulz (III.24). Critical opinion is divided as to Hoccleve's merits or demerits as a poet. The lack of agreement among scholars suggests that the last word has not been said. On almost all aspects of his poetic technique one can find critical judgments totally different. Some writers, beginning with Thomas Warton (IV.71), see little value in his verse; others, led by Bernhard ten Brink (IV.5), find much to praise. Hoccleve criticism leading to value judgments varies in depth and reliability. Some of the appraisals, like those by Hammond (IV.28) and Bennett (IV.2), are carefully thought out and quite perceptive: others are superficial, derivative, dogmatic, or prejudiced, and therefore undependable.

There are several aspects of Hoccleve's work to which scholars have constantly addressed themselves. Some have emphasized the importance of his verse as a storehouse of information on fifteenth-century society and politics. Others, concerned primarily with his relationship with Chaucer, have discussed the portrait of Chaucer in the *Regement of Princes* and have spoken admiringly of his supposedly heartfelt stanzas, in the same poem, lamenting the death of Chaucer. Hoccleve's meter has also been a subject of much discussion. Perhaps the main reason why his poetry is held in low repute today is that critical opinion of his versification has almost invariably been negative. Hoccleve has been accused of "meetrynge amis," that is, of placing verse accents on syllables normally unstressed and rapidly passing over syllables that should receive stress. Despite differences of opinion on the literary value of his poetry, most writers have found his autobiographical passages worthy of comment. The personal element is certainly the most distinctive feature of his verse; it sets it apart from the more conventional efforts of his contemporaries.

The present study, literary-historically oriented, examines Hoccleve's poetry in the context of other late medieval literature. It treats his poetry as a whole. Much of it is concerned, directly or indirectly, with the question of convention and individuality. The first chapter examines the autobiographical element in Hoccleve; it has been published separately, in a somewhat shorter version, in the September 1967 issue of the *Modern Language Quarterly*. The rest of the work concerns itself with such matters as Hoccleve's themes and genres, his style, his handling of source material, his meter, and finally his relationship with Chaucer. The second section of the chapter on Hoccleve and Chaucer — "Hoccleve's Supposed Friendship with Chaucer" — is published separately in *English Language Notes,* IV (September 1966), 9-12. I wish to thank the editors of the two journals mentioned for allowing me to reproduce here, with a few changes, material already in print.

Most of Hoccleve's poems do not have definite titles. I have therefore adopted with minor changes the titles used by Furnivall and Gollancz in the Early English Text Society edition of Hoccleve's complete works. Later editors of individual poems have occasionally introduced different titles. Any resulting confusion I have straightened out in the appended bibliography. I have generally referred to one of Hoccleve's religious poems as the *Legend of the Virgin and Her Sleeveless Garment,* this title being shorter than the one used by Gollancz. For the sake of simplicity and convenience I have italicized the name of every poem, regardless of its length. All my quotations from Hoccleve follow Furnivall's and Gollancz's texts; but since my work has nothing to do with textual problems, I have not reproduced the indications either of editorial emendations or of editorial expansions of scribal abbreviations. I spell Hoccleve's name with the *H,* since this is the form found in the autograph manuscripts.

It is a pleasure for me to express my indebtedness to the following persons for their generous aid and contributions of advice:

To Professor John L. Lievsay of Duke University, for helping me in various stages of my work, especially in the revision of Chapter I; to Professor Robert Van Kluyve, also of Duke University, for taking time from his own work to teach me the rudiments of paleography, so that I could transcribe the Anglo-Latin source of Hoccleve's *Tale of Jonathas*; to Professor Henry Noble MacCracken, President Emeritus of Vassar College, for a priceless, entertaining letter answering my inquiry about the poems in Egerton MS. 615; to Mr. H. C. Schulz, Curator of Manuscripts at the Huntington Library, for information regarding the Hoccleve manuscripts there; to Mr. A. I. Doyle, Keeper of Rare Books at the Durham University Library, for information regarding the history of Durham MS. Cosin V. III. 9; to Professor Karl Heinz Göller of the University of Göttingen, for allowing me to use the facilities of the Seminar für Englische Philologie at Göttingen during the summer of 1966, while I was preparing the final draft.

I must also thank the Deutscher Akademischer Austauschdienst for granting me a fellowship in 1961-62 to study medieval English at the University of Bonn. During my two semesters there I had the privilege of taking part in an unforgettable *Oberseminar* conducted by Professor Walter F. Schirmer. At this time I became interested in specializing in late Middle English literature. Professor Schirmer's excellent book on Lydgate has been a source of inspiration for me as well as an indispensable guide in the relatively unexplored area of fifteenth-century English poetic. I would like to express my particular gratitude to Professor Schirmer for reading my Duke University doctoral dissertation, from which the present study evolves, and for giving me valuable advice regarding the further research and extensive revision necessary before publication would be conceivable.

JEROME MITCHELL

CONTENTS

CHAPTER I

THE AUTOBIOGRAPHICAL ELEMENT

Much is known about the life of Thomas Hoccleve, both from his own personal reminiscences in the autobiographically oriented poems and from various scattered references in the Privy Council Proceedings, the Patent Rolls, the Pells Issue Rolls, the Close Rolls, and the Fine Rolls. He was born about 1368, perhaps in the village of Hockliffe in Bedfordshire. At the age of eighteen or nineteen he began working as a clerk in the office of the Privy Seal, and in this capacity he remained for about thirty-five years. During such time as he could spare from his drudging work he wrote poetry, his magnum opus being the *Regement of Princes,* which he dedicated to the Prince Hal later immortalized by Shakespeare. Despite the annuity granted to him in 1399, Hoccleve seems to have been beset with financial problems. In his poetry he often complains of a lack of funds and expresses his fear of being completely impoverished when old. Other personal matters with which he is much concerned are his misspent youth, his frustrating work in the Privy Seal, and his poor health. Hoccleve's name disappears from all official governmental records after 1426. He died probably about 1430.[1]

[1] The most convenient source of biographical information on Hoccleve other than his poems is Frederick J. Furnivall's "Appendix of Entries About Grants and Payments to Hoccleve, from the Privy-Council Proceedings, the Patent- and Issue-Rolls, and the Record Office," included in the prefatory material to his edition of Hoccleve's *Minor Poems,* E.E.T.S., E.S., No. 61 (London, 1892). A few additional items, most of which have been pointed out before in scattered places, comprise the second appendix to my unpublished doctoral dissertation, "Thomas Hoccleve: His Traditionalism and His Individuality: A Study in Fifteenth-Century English Poetic" (Duke, 1965). See also H. S. Bennett's chapter on Hoccleve in *Six Medieval Men and Women* (Cambridge, 1955). For the date of Hoccleve's death see H. C. Schulz, "Thomas Hoccleve, Scribe," *Speculum,* XII (1937), 76-81.

Many scholars have felt that the autobiographical element is the most interesting feature of Hoccleve's verse.[2] This chapter reexamines Hoccleve's autobiographical passages in relation to the work of his contemporaries and immediate predecessors and suggests that they reveal a degree of individuality unparalleled in Middle English poetry.

Details presumably relating to the poet's life crop up in many of his works, the most important and extensive of the autobiographical passages being found in *La Male Regle* (1406), the Prologue to the *Regement of Princes* (1412), the *Complaint* (1422), and the *Dialogue with a Friend* (1422).[3] The dates, fairly accurate, have been arrived at through calculations based on references Hoccleve makes to his own age in the poems themselves. He wrote *La Male Regle* when he was a relatively young man and still a novice in the art of poetry; he wrote the Prologue to the *Regement* in middle age; and he wrote the *Complaint* and the *Dialogue* some five years after his bout with an emotional disorder which bordered on insanity. Thus the poems span Hoccleve's entire productive period.

Just how much of what Hoccleve says in his first-person narratives is really true, and how much is pseudo-autobiographical, and how much is pure convention is a question not easily answered. Much ink has been spilt on the same problem as it is found in Chaucer's dream poems. Fortunately, the question of Hoccleve's *persona* is not so complex as that of Chaucer's, since in this case matters are not further complicated by the machinery of the dream poem. Yet the basic problem remains. To what extent can the "I" of the so-called autobiographical poems be identified with Hoccleve himself? To what extent can the autobiographical passages be regarded as genuine, individualized self-revelation? Almost all Hoccleve's critics have accepted these passages at their face value. In some instances the poet's entire life has been reconstructed from them. Indeed, the only writer to question Hoccleve's veracity was G. Gregory Smith,

[2] See my Hoccleve bibliography, especially Section IV, *passim*. Hoccleve's literary reputation is discussed at length in the first chapter of my doctoral dissertation (see n. 1 above).

[3] *La Male Regle,* the *Complaint,* and the *Dialogue* are included in Furnivall's edition of the *Minor Poems.* The *Regement of Princes,* also edited by Furnivall, is a separate issue: E.E.T.S., E.S., No. 72 (London, 1897). Hoccleve's *Minor Poems* in Huntington Libr. MS. HM 744 (*olim* Ashburnham MS. Addit. 133) are edited by Sir Israel Gollancz: E.E.T.S., E.S., No. 73 (London, 1925 [for 1897]). All quotations from Hoccleve follow these texts.

who believed that the so-called personal element in Hoccleve (and in Lydgate) was "more conventional and rhetorical, and of a pattern, than individual."[4]

Smith's observations cannot be dismissed lightly. Much of what Hoccleve tells us about himself cannot be substantiated with any existing official records. In the Prologue to the *Regement of Princes* (vv. 1447 ff.) he tells the Beggar that he intended to be a priest and waited long for a benefice. When it seemed clear that none was forthcoming, he married, even though he had second thoughts about losing his freedom as a bachelor. In the *Dialogue with a Friend* he refers again to his wife. Yet there are no official records to back up his remarks regarding either his marriage or his thwarted intention to become a priest. What Hoccleve has said may be true, but we do not know for certain. In addition to passages which cannot be verified with other sources of information there are other "autobiographical" passages which have a decidedly conventional ring. Smith cites the *Complaint* and the *Dialogue* as examples. Possibly the conventional element is even more pronounced in the opening stanzas of the Prologue to the *Regement,* in which Hoccleve broods on the misery in the world, the capriciousness of Fortune, and his own emotional turmoil. There is one personal touch — his reference to his dwelling "at Chestre ynne"; but there is certainly nothing individual either in the ideas presented or in the general situation. Similar passages can be found in other Middle English poems. Chaucer's *Book of the Duchess,* for instance, begins in much the same fashion.

Some of the details in the "autobiographical" poems are seemingly contradicted by known facts. For one thing, Hoccleve incessantly complains about his straitened financial circumstances both in these poems and in the short poems of solicitation, such as the *Balade to My Lord the Chancellor,* the *Balade and Roundel to Mr. Henry Somer,* the *Balade to King Henry V for Money,* and the *Balade to My Maister Carpenter.* Yet the records show that Hoccleve was not so hard up as he would have us believe. In November 1399 he was granted an annuity of £10 for life, and this was increased in May 1409 to 20 marks (£13 6*s.* 8*d.*) — no mean sum for a scrivener in the early fifteenth century.[5] Hoccleve was paid semiannually and, apparently, with some degree of regularity. In addition, he derived money from sources other than his regular income. On one occasion

[4] *The Transition Period* (Edinburgh and London, 1900), pp. 19-20.
[5] Furnivall's "Appendix," pp. li, lvii.

he and three of his fellow clerks divided £40 worth of goods confiscated from outlaws.[6] It seems, then, that there is a certain amount of conventional poverty in Hoccleve's frequent complaints to his empty purse. Similar poems can be found among the works of Chaucer and Lydgate.

In the *Complaint* and the *Dialogue,* probably written in 1422, Hoccleve discusses at some length the emotional disorder or insanity which he experienced five years previously. Exactly how long the sickness lasted he does not say, but he implies a substantial period of time — perhaps weeks, perhaps months. When, as he puts it, the substance of his memory finally returned from play, he had great difficulty in being admitted once again into the fellowship of his former friends, who were mistakenly convinced that his madness would return. But the poet's own words are the only record we have of his sickness; the official governmental documents make no mention of it. Moreover, during the time of his supposed madness and the period immediately following it, Hoccleve drew his annuity regularly, sometimes "by his own hands."[7] It seems odd that there should be no other record of his illness if it was really so severe and so noticeable to others as he would have us believe.

So much for the questionable autobiographical details. On the other side of the picture — something not considered by Gregory Smith — there are many autobiographical details that are verifiable. Hoccleve refers several times to his work in the office of the Privy Seal. In *La Male Regle* he tells us that none of his colleagues "in al the priuee seel" ever drank so much as he (vv. 307-308). In the Prologue to the *Regement of Princes* he alludes to the length of time he has served as a scrivener (vv. 801-805). He also tells the Beggar the amount of his annuity — 20 marks — the figure agreeing perfectly with the official records (vv. 820-822). A few lines later he expatiates on the many inconveniences encountered by professional scribes (vv. 988 ff.). In the *Complaint* he writes that his former friends would often ask his "fellawes / of the prive seale" about the state of his health (vv. 295-298). Finally, in a few of the autobiographical passages Hoccleve refers to himself by name. At first glance this would seem a trivial point; but in some of the most cele-

[6] Bennett, p. 82.
[7] Furnivall's "Appendix," pp. lxiii-lxiv.

brated medieval "autobiographical" poems (such as *The Kingis Quair*) the "I" never identifies himself.

We are not able, then, to dismiss Hoccleve's work as pure convention, Gregory Smith notwithstanding. Smith's remarks are also open to debate because he equates Hoccleve's autobiographical passages with what he believes to be similar passages in Lydgate's *Testament.* I shall attempt to show later that the autobiographical passages in the *Testament* differ in several important respects from those in Hoccleve. What the two poets have done is not so similar as might appear at first glance. Finally, although Smith implies that no complete study of fifteenth-century "anticipations" of the personal quality characteristic of later times has ever been made, he gives the impression that Hoccleve's type of work, especially *La Male Regle,* was common in medieval times. This, it seems to me, is another very questionable point.

In medieval *English* poetry indisputably genuine autobiographical passages are exceptional. Even in the years immediately preceding Hoccleve's productive period — an age which in all respects was the high-water mark of Middle English poetry — autobiographical allusions are extremely rare. We know, for example, really nothing at all about the life of the Pearl Poet from his works. It may be that *Pearl* was based on a personal experience, the untimely death of the poet's own daughter, but more than this we cannot say. Langland refers vaguely to himself in a few places, notably in the sixth passus of the C-text of *Piers Plowman.* At one point he tells Conscience that in past years he had his "tyme mysspended" (Skeat text, C.VI. 93); but unlike Hoccleve he gives no specific details. Gower also has very little to say about himself that could not be labeled pure convention. There is perhaps no reason to doubt his account, in the first version of the Prologue to the *Confessio Amantis,* of his meeting Richard II on the Thames and his receiving the King's suggestions for a new book (Macaulay text, vv. 34-53). But one learns almost nothing about the man John Gower from these lines; the personal touch is lacking. Even in the poetry of Chaucer there are very few clearly autobiographical passages, and most of these occur in one poem, the *House of Fame.* It seems, however, that Chaucer's work in this vein, although slight, may have had some influence on Hoccleve. The matter will deserve our closer attention later.

The poets of Hoccleve's own day do not talk about themselves except in general terms. Writing in 1406 or 1407 Henry Scogan has one stanza in his *Moral Balade*[8] (a poem of 189 lines) which might be labeled autobiographical:

> I complayn sore, whan I remembre me
> The sodeyn age that is upon me falle;
> More I complayn my mispent juventè
> The whiche is impossible ayein to calle.
> But certainly, the most complaynte of alle
> Is for to thinke, that I have been so nyce
> That I ne wolde no virtue to me calle
> In al my youthe, but vyces ay cheryce.
>
> [vv. 9-16]

Scogan appears to be much concerned about his misspent youth, but he is unwilling to reveal what his vices were. Whether he drank excessively, or deflowered young (or old) maidens or robbed wayfarers on the king's highway, or committed more serious (or less serious) offenses, we simply cannot say. The poem lacks specific detail, as do most of the other fifteenth-century "autobiographical" poems. *The Kingis Quair,*[9] for example, supposedly written by James I of Scotland during his imprisonment in England, has often been admired as an early specimen of autobiographical poetry. But even if one accepts the tradition that James was the author — and this is very questionable — the celebrated passages of self-revelation are not numerous and not at all explicit. In a poem consisting of 197 rhyme-royal stanzas, perhaps five stanzas might be called autobiographical. In stanzas xxii-xxv the poet writes that when he was three years past the state of innocence his guardians, for reasons unmentioned, advised him to leave the country. During the journey by sea he and his party were captured by enemies and taken by force to a strange country. There he was put into a "strong prisoun," where he was to remain for twice nine years. This well-known section of the poem may refer to an episode in the life of King James, but whoever wrote it obviously intended for it to be vague. Certain basic facts are not related to us. We do not know, for example, who the "I" is. Nor do we know what country he is from, or what land he is bound for, or who his enemies are, or where he is imprisoned. Adjacent to the prison there is a garden, described in stanzas xxxi-xxxiii. One cannot help wondering whether this is a real garden or rather a

[8] Included in *Chaucerian and Other Pieces,* ed. Walter W. Skeat (Oxford, 1897), pp. 237-244.

[9] Ed. Walter W. Skeat, Scottish Text Soc., N.S., No. 1 (Edinburgh and London, 1911).

product of the poet's knowledge of medieval descriptions of ideal gardens so typical of dream poems. At stanza xl the narrator looks out of his prison window and sees a young lady (walking in the garden) with whom he immediately falls in love. This stanza too has been interpreted as straight autobiography and pointed out as an early example of love at first sight. Yet the name of the lady is not given anywhere in the poem. W. MacKay McKenzie finds no indication in the historical records that King James ever fell in love at first sight from a tower window.[10]

Autobiographical passages are not to be found either in John Walton's verse translation of Boethius' *Consolation of Philosophy* or in the poetical works of John Capgrave — although in the latter's prose histories, it should be noted, a few personal allusions do occur.[11] Things are different with Osbern Bokenham[12] and George Ashby,[13] two relatively obscure poets who flourished in the years immediately following Hoccleve's death. In the works of both men occasional autobiographical passages can be pointed out. In Bokenham they occur mainly in the General Prologue to his *Legendys of Hooly Wummen* and in "The prolocutorye in-to Marye Mawdelyns lyf." In the General Prologue he alludes briefly to the last time he was in Italy (vv. 107 ff.). He notes that the relics of St. Margaret are kept at a priory near the place where he was born, and he comments on some of the miracles performed by means of them (vv. 133 ff.). Once while he was in Venice, he managed to avoid misfortune and possible death through a miracle owing to these relics. Several wicked men had thrown him from his barge into a fen and were about to leave him to his fate. They allowed him to come back on board when he promised to bring them a ring with which he had touched St. Margaret's bare foot (vv. 157-172). His apparently sincere account of the incident reveals an aspect of the medieval frame of mind quite alien to modern temperament. But the passage is memorable mainly because of the poet's use of specific detail — something almost totally lacking in the so-called autobiographical

[10] See the introduction to his edition of *The Kingis Quair* (London, [1937]), pp. 15-16.

[11] See Francis Charles Hingeston's introduction to Capgrave's *Chronicle of England* (London, 1858), pp. xi-xii.

[12] *Legendys of Hooly Wummen,* ed. Mary S. Serjeantson, E.E.T.S., O.S., No. 206 (London, 1938 [for 1936]).

[13] *George Ashby's Poems,* ed. Mary Bateson, E.E.T.S., E.S., No. 76 (London, 1899).

passages of Scogan and King James. In "The prolocutorye in-to Marye Mawdelyns lyf" Bokenham describes a visit he paid to Lady Isabel Bourchier, Countess of Eu, and the discussion which they had regarding his metrical legends, while her

> . . . foure sonys ying
> Besy were wyth reuel & wyth daunsyng,
> And oþere mo in þere most fressh aray
> Dysgysyd . . .
>
> [vv. 5023-26]

This passage too owes its effectiveness to specific detail and, a few lines later, to the poet's use of direct discourse. Bokenham's passages of self-revelation comprise a relatively small segment of his nearly 11,000 verses. They can certainly be compared with the autobiographical material in Hoccleve; but Hoccleve's work in this vein is much more extensive and, as I shall attempt to show, more convincing and more minutely detailed. As for Ashby, the opening stanzas of *A Prisoner's Reflections* are apparently autobiographical. Ashby has been thrown into the Fleet "by a gret commaundment of a lord" (v. 9); he gives us his name; he laments that he has been forsaken by his old friends; he is unable to get out of debt. He spent his best years in the service of Henry VI, Margaret of Anjou, and their uncle, the Duke of Gloucester; and now, in his old age, Fortune has turned against him. Ashby's account of his troubles is sincere enough, but most of what he says could be said by many a prisoner. That is, his stanzas of self-revelation lack individuality; they convey almost nothing of their author's personality. Ashby has not managed (or perhaps not even attempted) to characterize himself.

Essentially the same thing can be said about the autobiographical material in Part IV of Lydgate's *Testament.*[14] As a boy Lydgate hated school; he disputed with his friends; he told lies; he had no respect for his betters; and, worst of all, he stole apples from the monastery garden and grapes from a neighboring vineyard. After he became a novice he drank too much, listened to "veyn fables," came to prayers late, took small comfort in holy histories, and complained about the monastery food. At the age of fifteen his sinful life came to an abrupt end when he saw, painted on a wall of the monastery, a mysterious crucifix, with words beside it admonishing

[14] Included in *The Minor Poems of John Lydgate,* ed. Henry Noble MacCracken, Pt. 1, E.E.T.S., E.S., No. 107 (London, 1911 [for 1910]), pp. 329-362.

him to leave his pride. Despite the length of the section (147 lines) and the multitude of autobiographical allusions, Lydgate has not given his *Testament* the personal touch he might have. One reason for the lack of individuality is that he chooses to give many short allusions to his childhood days, one after another, instead of limiting himself to a few points and elaborating on these. One stanza will illustrate my point:

> I had in custome to come to skole late,
> Nat for to lerne but for a contenaunce,
> With my felawes redy to debate,
> To Iangle or Iape was sett all my pleasaunce;
> Wherof rebuked this was my chevesaunce,
> To forge a lesyng, and thervpon to muse,
> Whanne I trespaced, my-selven to excuse.
> [vv. 628-634]

The details summarily presented here could have been developed much more fully. Lydgate might have described, for example, a specific occasion on which he arrived at school late. He might have given the exact words that passed between himself and his comrades during their arguments. He might have told us some of the lies he concocted, and he might have described a specific incident in which he tried to lie his way out of some wrong he had committed. But because he has not developed the autobiographical material by describing specific incidents, his confessions apply to almost any childhood.

None of the writers discussed so far wrote autobiographical passages very similar to those of Hoccleve. Before examining Hoccleve's work, however, we must return to Chaucer, especially his *House of Fame*. It is sometimes difficult to draw a line between what are autobiographical allusions and what are not; but three or four passages almost certainly reflect Chaucer's own life. Near the beginning of Book II, for instance, the poet makes what is probably a humorous allusion to his wife Philippa. When the eagle says to him, "Awak!" he is reminded of one he could name, who often awakened him with the same word, but not so gently (Robinson text, vv. 554-566). Several lines later occurs reference to Chaucer's physical appearance. The eagle says,

> "Seynte Marye!
> Thou art noyous for to carye,
> And nothyng nedeth it, pardee!"
> [vv. 573-575]

We know, of course, from pictures of Chaucer that have come down to us — including Hoccleve's famous portrait (see Chapter VI, Section 1) — that he was short in stature, but rather thickset. The most interesting autobiographical allusion is the well-known passage in which we catch a glimpse of Chaucer's life when he was Controller of the Customs (vv. 641-660). Finally, in line 729 the eagle calls Chaucer by his given name, "Geffrey." The direct discourse Chaucer uses in all four instances makes the autobiographical allusions livelier in tone, more realistic and lifelike in their impact upon an audience or a reader — in a word, more convincing. Another prominent aspect of Chaucer's autobiographical material is its humor — something totally lacking in the work of Bokenham, Ashby, Lydgate, and the others. Finally, Chaucer has managed to convey something of his own personality in these brief passages. Somehow the lines bear his individual stamp. There is no question of the allusions being couched in general terms that would apply to almost anyone. The autobiographical element in Chaucer is very scanty; but Hoccleve apparently took a hint from Chaucer and developed his own autobiographical technique along the lines suggested in the *House of Fame.*

La Male Regle, the Prologue to the *Regement of Princes*, the *Complaint*, and the *Dialogue with a Friend* differ from each other in subject matter, presentation of material, and tone; but the autobiographical element is prominent in all four works. Indeed, it is the most striking feature. *La Male Regle*, perhaps Hoccleve's best-known poem (if the frequent number of times selections from it appear in anthologies is any indication of its fame), consists of fifty-six eight-line stanzas of pentameter with a rhyme scheme of *ababbcbc*. Interestingly, Hoccleve wrote *La Male Regle* at approximately the same time that Scogan wrote *A Moral Balade.* Both poems are didactic; both are in eight-line stanzas. But instead of merely alluding, like Scogan, to his misspent youth, Hoccleve relates his youthful follies in detail.

The poem opens with an invocation to the god Health (sts. i-viii), wherein Hoccleve contrasts the health that he took for granted in his youth with his present bodily infirmities. The invocation is followed by a thoroughly conventional digression on Youth and Reason (sts. ix-xi) — Youth representing unrestraint, nonconformity, and folly, and Reason the opposite qualities. The next division (sts. xii-xxvi) is apparently autobiographical. If some of the details are not actually true, one would never know the difference, for Hoccleve has a knack of making all his autobiographical allusions seem genuine. He begins by talking in general terms about his misspent youth, but he gradually becomes more specific. The series of intimate confessions gets under way in stanza xvi with a brief description of the "signe of Bachus," which lures the poet into a London tavern. In each stanza hereafter, Hoccleve has painted a miniature self-portrait. He has made each stanza memorable by means of specific, descriptive details and through intimate, unabashed remarks about his own rather effeminate personality. He chases after girls at "Poules heed" (st. xviii) ; he treats them to wine and wafers (st. xix) ; he likes them to kiss him (v. 155) ; and he is as content with a kiss as he would have been "with the deede" (v. 156). "Of loues aart," he writes, "yit touchid I no deel" (v. 153). When men speak of sexual matters in his presence, he waxes "as reed as is the gleede" (v. 159). Afraid of fighting, he either keeps his mouth shut or whispers bad things about a person behind his back (st. xxii). He pays the taverners and the cooks at Westminster gate so well that they think he is "a verray gentil man" (st. xxiii). After a visit to the tavern he often takes a boat ride, tipping the boatmen lavishly and being highly pleased when they call him "maistir" (sts. xxiv-xxvi). On this personal note the first autobiographical section ends.

The next division consists of a conventional didactic discourse on the troubles which befall men when they listen to flatterers. Then, at stanza xxxix, Hoccleve returns to an account of his misspent youth. He describes amusingly his unwillingness to get out of bed on the morning after a night of debauchery. Only his two fellow clerks, Prentys and Arondel, are worse offenders than he. Sometimes they sleep until "it drawith ny the pryme" (see vv. 317-326). Next, in an apostrophe to himself (vv. 351 ff.), Hoccleve alludes to his want of money. In the last part of the poem he implores the god Health to see to it that Lord Fourneval, the treasurer, pay his overdue annuity of £10. The figure is correct, according to the official governmental records (see n. 5 above). By asking the god Health to intercede for him, Hoccleve is able to beg for his annuity in a manner that does not seem offensively overt.

La Male Regle obviously contains some conventional subject matter, such as the discourse on Youth and Reason, the sermon on flattery, and the plea for money. Even the idea of a misspent youth is nothing unusual. But the foregoing summary suggests that Hoccleve's *handling* of autobiographical material is quite different from that of the writers discussed earlier. Even though Hoccleve has not experimented with direct discourse in *La Male Regle,* he has made the autobiographical passages vivid and memorable by the use of specific detail. He makes a point of telling us exactly *how* he misspent his youth by describing, with a few well-chosen details, certain aspects of his personal life instead of simply mentioning or listing them. The humorous tone of some of the passages is also a factor not to be overlooked. Like Chaucer, Hoccleve has managed to give his passages of self-revelation an individual stamp. A real human personality emerges from the pages of *La Male Regle* — a personality which we can watch develop and observe in different circumstances in the Prologue to the *Regement,* the *Complaint,* and the *Dialogue.*

The opening stanzas of the Prologue to the *Regement* are, as I have remarked earlier, quite conventional. The *persona* finds himself in a typical medieval intellectual dilemma. He cannot sleep. He meditates on the capriciousness of Fortune — so well exemplified in the recent case of Richard II — and concludes pessimistically that inconstancy rules the world. Only a person who has nothing is safe from the wiles of Fortune, but such a person is already miserable. The narrator sees no purpose in striving and begins to look forward to death. In this frame of mind he goes out the next morning into the fields and encounters an old beggar. Again the situation is conventional. Sometimes such old men are symbolic of Reason or Wisdom (like Virgil in the *Divine Comedy*) and sometimes of Death (like the old man in Chaucer's Pardoner's Tale). Indeed, the conflict between Youth and Age is a leitmotiv in medieval literature. Many writers seem to have felt that old men had somehow solved the riddle of human existence, that they had discovered the meaningful life.

With all these ideas in the background the scene is suddenly brought to life as the Beggar awakens Hoccleve from his reverie:

> He sterte vp to me, & seyde, "scleepys þou, man?
> Awake!" & gan me schake wonder faste,
> And with a sigh I answerde atte laste.
>
> "A! who is þer?" "I," quod þis olde greye,
> "Am heer," & he me tolde the manere
> How he spak to me, as ye herd me seye;
> "O man," quoþ I, "for cristes loue dere,
> If þat þou wolt aght done at my preyere,

As go þi way, talke to me no more,
Þi wordes al annoyen me ful sore;

"Voyde fro me; me list no compaignye;
Encresse noght my grife; I haue I-now."
[vv. 131-142]

But the talkative old man has no intention of leaving and, humorously enough, imposes himself on the melancholy poet when he is in no mood to be disturbed. The lively, realistic dialogue is typical of many places in the Prologue. Indeed, Hoccleve has made it a consistent practice to interrupt the Beggar's long didactic sermons either with lively repartee or with passages of self-revelation.

The material of the Prologue to the *Regement* has no well-defined organization. The conversation rambles on from one topic to another. The first passage of self-revelation comes not from Hoccleve but from the Beggar (vv. 610 ff.). The Beggar's account of his misspent youth resembles in many respects Hoccleve's account of himself in *La Male Regle*. In his youth the Beggar, like Hoccleve, spent too much of his time in taverns. He shied away from all physical violence; but unlike Hoccleve he seems often to have "done the deed" with females, whether they were maids, wives, or even nuns. Eventually he ran out of money and was forsaken by his friends.

At line 750 Hoccleve begins a long passage of self-revelation in which he tells the Beggar the cause of his melancholy. He is in straitened financial circumstances and fears he will be destitute in his old age. During the course of his long-winded complaint he digresses on the English soldiers who once fought gloriously in France but who were now back home — old, penniless, and friendless (vv. 869 ff.). He fears that his plight will be the same as theirs unless his annuity is paid. Probably, as I suggested earlier, Hoccleve was never so destitute as he pretends in this "autobiographical" passage. On the other hand, his references to his work in the Privy Seal (v. 802), the length of his service (vv. 804-805), and the exact amount of his annuity (v. 822) *are* true and can be substantiated with the official records. His complaint contains just enough truth to seem plausible as a whole.

In stanzas cxlii-cxlvii Hoccleve comments vividly on the troubles and tribulations encountered by scribes. Their work is more difficult than it would seem to the casual observer. The passage owes much of its effectiveness to specific detail, as the following stanzas suggest:

"Wrytyng also doth grete annoyes thre,
Of which ful fewe folkes taken heede
Sauf we oure self; and thise, lo, þei be:
Stomak is on, whom stowpyng out of dreede
Annoyeth soore; and to our bakkes, neede
Mot it be greuous; and þe thrid, our yen,
Vp-on þe whyte mochel sorwe dryen.

"What man þat thre & twenti yeere and more
In wryting hath continued, as haue I,
I dar wel seyn it smerteth hym ful sore
In euere veyne and place of his body;
And yen moost it greeueth trewely
Of any crafte þat man can ymagyne:
ffadir, in feth, it spilt hath wel ny myne."
[vv. 1016-29]

H. C. Schulz, taking Hoccleve's words at face value, offers the poet's poor eyesight as one explanation for some of the errors in the autograph manuscripts.[15] The entire section on clerical work is reminiscent of the passage in the *House of Fame* in which the eagle refers to Chaucer's bookwork — although Hoccleve's treatment of the subject, to be sure, is much more detailed.

Other passages of self-revelation include the poet's allusions to his wife (vv. 1226, 1453-56, 1560-61) and his discussion (vv. 1499-1547) of the mistreatment which the clerks of the Privy Seal experience in their dealings with servants of important lords. The servants take for themselves money which their lords intended for the clerks. And the clerks dare not bring the matter into the open for fear of being punished, because the evil servants would never admit that they had pocketed the money for themselves. After a lengthy didactic section on marriage, the conversation returns to Hoccleve's fear that his annuity will not be paid (vv. 1779 ff.) ; and a few lines later the Beggar suggests that he appeal to Prince Henry for help (vv. 1842 ff.). The last passage of self-revelation is one of the often quoted passages in which Hoccleve laments the death of Chaucer (vv. 1958-74). He refers briefly to Gower at verse 1975 and then apologizes for his own shortcomings as a poet (vv. 1982-86) in what is probably a bit of conventional self-deprecation. Sud-

[15] "Thomas Hoccleve, Scribe," p. 76. Schulz argues convincingly that Huntington Libr. MS. HM 111 (*olim* Phillipps MS. 8151), Huntington Libr. MS. HM 744 (*olim* Ashburnham MS. Addit. 133), Durham MS. Cosin V. III. 9, and Brit. Mus. MS. Addit. 24062 are autograph manuscripts. Interestingly, Hoccleve is the only significant Middle English writer whose works have in large part been preserved in autograph manuscripts.

denly the Beggar announces to Hoccleve that he must go. He and the poet quickly take leave of one another, and the long, rambling Prologue to the *Regement of Princes* ends.

The foregoing discussion suggests some of the ways in which the Prologue to the *Regement,* as an autobiographical poem, differs from the work of other medieval poets. Hoccleve has written passages of self-revelation which are much longer than those of other writers; he has mixed known facts with conventional material in such a way that the whole seems true; he has used lively, realistic dialogue throughout; he makes a point of giving specific details; he describes fully various aspects of his life; and, finally, he has the knack of revealing his own feelings convincingly. The personality that emerges from the Prologue to the *Regement* is that of a weak, timorous, self-centered, but very human individual.

Hoccleve's *Complaint* and the *Dialogue with a Friend* have received less attention than they deserve and have been printed in their entirety only once — in Furnivall's edition of the *Minor Poems.* The Prologue to the *Complaint* is reminiscent of the opening stanzas of the Prologue to the *Regement of Princes*; but Hoccleve succeeds, more than in the earlier poem, in giving the impression of sincerity, despite the conventional element. The first stanza is remarkable as one of the few examples of nature description in Hoccleve's works. The poet sees in the dying year a reflection of his own depressed spirits. He cannot sleep; he has found himself out of favor *since his last sickness*; and he longs for death. Hoccleve's sickness is the subject of the *Complaint* — a work extremely interesting from a psychological standpoint because it is the only Middle English poem of self-revelation in which an author analyzes the symptoms of a severe emotional disorder he once experienced. And if this in itself does not make the *Complaint* unique, Hoccleve also discusses his difficulty in readjusting himself to normal life and comments on the reactions of his friends both during the illness and after his recovery.

Like the Prologue to the *Regement,* the *Complaint* has no well-defined organization. Hoccleve rambles from one point to another, apparently simply putting down his thoughts as they come to him. Unlike the earlier work, however, the *Complaint* does contain one unifying element — the subject of the poet's illness. Everything relates to this one central theme. Hoccleve looks back on his illness as a time when, as he puts it, the substance of his memory went to play (vv. 50-51). After he had recovered, five years prior to the time when he actually wrote the *Complaint*, his friends would not readmit him into their company. They even made a conscious practice of avoiding him, and they believed that his recovery was only temporary. Hoccleve records some of their remarks:

> "all-thowghe from hym / his siknesse savage
> with-drawne and passyd / as for a tyme be,
> Resorte it wole / namely in suche age
> as he is of" . . .
> [vv. 86-89]
>
> "whane passinge hete is," quod they, "trustyth this,
> assaile hym wole agayne that maladie."
> [vv. 92-93]

He then observes that men should not pretend to be wiser than they really are. Only God knows what the future holds. It was God who visited him and afflicted him with "that wildenesse" (v. 107) when he least expected it.

At this point Hoccleve recalls a few of the incidents which happened during the actual time of his illness. He writes that his friends observed him closely and discussed among themselves the outward manifestations of his disorder:

> Men seyden, I loked / as a wilde steer,
> and so my loke abowt I gan to throwe;
> myne heed to hie / a-nother seide I beer,
> ful bukkyshe is his brayne / well may I trowe;
> and seyde the thirde / and apt is in the rowe
> to site of them / that a resounles reed
> Can geve / no sadnesse is in his heed.
>
> Chaungid had I my pas / some seiden eke,
> for here and there / forthe stirte I as a Roo,
> none abode / none arrest, but all brain-seke,
> A-nother spake / and of me seide also,
> my feete weren aye / wavynge to and fro
> whane that I stonde shulde / and withe men talke,
> and that myne eyne / sowghten every halke.
> [vv. 120-133]

Hoccleve was unable to answer the allegations of his friends because of a speech difficulty that accompanied his illness—"I hadd lost my tonges key" (v. 144). In the privacy of his home he would look at his face in a mirror but could find no change in his physical appearance. He did not know whether to be seen on the streets when he was out of favor or to stay at home and run the risk of being held more seriously ill than he really was (vv. 183 ff.). Finally his memory returned. In the remaining part of the poem he discusses his feelings about the present state of his mind, his difficulty in being accepted once again by his friends, his near surrender of himself to utter despair, and his final religious solution to his problems.

How much of Hoccleve's rambling discourse is true one cannot say for certain, since there is nothing in any of the existing governmental documents to indicate that the poet ever suffered from a mental breakdown. But Hoccleve's account of his illness, whether entirely true or not, is certainly most convincing. The detail with which he describes various aspects of his malady, the apparent sincerity with which he relates certain incidents and his feelings toward them — all these qualities make the *Complaint* seem very real; while the subject matter alone makes it a unique Middle English poem of self-revelation.

The *Dialogue with a Friend* immediately follows the *Complaint* in Durham MS. Cosin V. III. 9 (the holograph on which Furnivall's text is based). The first two stanzas exemplify the colloquial, natural, unadorned style that Hoccleve uses in most of the poem's direct discourse:

> And, endyd my "complaynt" / in this manere,
> one knocked / at my chambre dore sore,
> and cryed a-lowde / "howe, hoccleve! arte thow here?
> open thy dore / me thinkethe it full yore
> sythen I the se / what, man, for goddes ore
> come out / for this quartar I not the sy,
> by owght I wot" / and out to hym cam I.
>
> This man was my good frynde / of farn a-gon,
> that I speke of / and thus he to me seyde:
> "Thomas / as thow me lovest, tell a-non
> what dydist thow / when I knocked and leyde
> so fast upon thy dore" / And I obeyde
> vnto his will / "come in," quod I, "and se."
> and so he dyd / he streyght went in with me.
>
> [vv. 1-14]

There are fewer long speeches in the *Dialogue with a Friend* than in the Prologue to the *Regement of Princes*, and the dialogue frequently moves back and forth within a single stanza — sometimes even within a single line. The casual, freely moving discourse gives a realistic touch to the autobiographical material presented.

The *Dialogue with a Friend* cannot be summarized easily because of the great diversity of its subject matter. It can be best described as a pleasant metrical hodgepodge of varying moods and ideas. Between the half-serious, half-affected melancholy that is prevalent as Hoccleve broods on the world's perennial sorrows (vv. 246-287) and the good-humored fun to be found in the section on women (vv. 715-826) — a section that reveals the poet's feminist sympathies — there is a middle ground where Hoccleve and his friend bandy ideas on various subjects. Hoccleve inveighs against coin-clippers in a passage that reveals his interest in a serious social and political problem of the times (vv. 99-196); he digresses on friendship, having nothing original to add to the time-worn subject (vv. 323-364); and he sings the praises of Humphrey, Duke of Gloucester, in a *topos* involving the eulogy of a great man (vv. 554-623). The last two items are largely conventional; the others reveal something of the poet's personality. The most important theme of the *Dialogue*, however, reveals much of Hoccleve's own personality. As in the *Complaint*, the predominant theme is autobiographical, namely, the question of Hoccleve's sanity. Hoccleve wants to translate a Latin treatise on the art of dying, but his friend objects. He is afraid that the poet has not recovered sufficiently from his nervous disorder to engage in work that would require much mental exertion. Many arguments for and against Hoccleve's resumption of his efforts in verse are amicably exchanged, until the friend is thoroughly convinced that the poet is in control of his mental faculties. If the *Dialogue* has a *raison d'être*, it may be simply that Hoccleve felt a need to prove to himself that his mind was stable and that he was capable of writing poetry once again.

Whether they should be taken at face value or not, the passages of self-revelation are convincing, and they *are* so for the same reasons that the other poems are convincing. A great deal of Hoccleve's personality is revealed in the pleasant, chatty direct discourse. The *Dialogue* is a mellow poem. There are no unpleasant emotional outbursts, no passages of impassioned rhetoric, no woeful appeals for money. The *Dialogue* gives the appearance of having been written by an older man — or at least a man who has come to terms with the world. In its rambling movement from one mood and idea to another, the poem has the flavor of an informal essay.

A clear, individualized portrait of Thomas Hoccleve emerges from the pages of *La Male Regle*, the Prologue to the *Regement of Princes*, the *Complaint*, and the *Dialogue with a Friend*. If the portrait is not flattering in all instances, it is certainly very human. Hoccleve's passages of self-revelation are longer and more numerous

than those of any other medieval English poet. In a complex self-portrait, sheer bulk is an important factor; but it is not the only one. Hoccleve succeeds mainly through his willingness to describe fully, with specific details, various aspects of his life and his feelings toward them. His use of lively, colloquial, good-humored direct discourse gives his work a decidedly realistic touch. Few Middle English poems contain autobiographical passages comparable to those of Hoccleve in realism, individuality, and apparent sincerity.

CHAPTER II

THEMES AND GENRES

Hoccleve wrote approximately 13,000 lines of poetry. From the standpoint of sheer bulk his work seems insignificant beside that of Lydgate, who wrote over ten times as much. But despite the relatively small amount Hoccleve's work is highly representative of fifteenth-century taste in poetry. Hoccleve tried his hand at a number of well-known genres and concerned himself with themes that were of current interest throughout the late Middle Ages. His work reveals that he was very much a product of his age. Except for the autobiographical poems, both his subject matter and his ways of handling it show clearly the trappings of convention. Yet Hoccleve sometimes managed to give even his most conventional work an individual touch — something that sets it apart from other fifteenth-century verse. In addition, he introduced into English some of the best-known traditional genres of late medieval literature.

1. COURTLY POETRY

One of Hoccleve's earliest works, the *Letter of Cupid,* is a courtly poem. The final stanza indicates that it was written in 1402. Based on Christine de Pisan's *Epistre au Dieu d'Amours* (1399), the *Letter* is a witty defense of women against the machinations of subtle clerks and false, slanderous lovers. It is thus an excellent example of medieval feminist literature and is, of course, diametrically opposed to such works as Walter Map's *Epistola Valerii ad Rufinum de non Ducenda Uxore,* Theophrastus' *Liber de Nuptiis,* St. Jerome's *Epistola Adversus Jovinianum,* and the other choice items bound up together in the book once belonging to Jankyn, the Wife of Bath's fifth husband.[1]

[1] See F. N. Robinson's notes to the Wife of Bath's Prologue in his second edition of *The Works of Geoffrey Chaucer* (Boston, 1957), pp. 698, 701.

Courtly poetry was an important genre in English literature from the time of Chaucer to the end of the fifteenth century;[2] and it has long been recognized that the English poems owe much to earlier French models, such as the *Roman de la Rose* and the works of Machaut, Deschamps, and Froissart. The genre is well represented in English by Chaucer's dream poems and by several fifteenth-century works. Some of the titles that come immediately to mind are Lydgate's four courtly poems: the *Flower of Courtesy* (ca. 1401), the *Complaint of the Black Knight* (ca. 1402), the *Temple of Glass* (ca. 1403), and *Reason and Sensuality* (ca. 1408); Sir Thomas Clanvowe's *Cuckoo and the Nightingale* (ca. 1403); Sir Richard Roos's *La Belle Dame sans Merci* (ca. 1460) — a translation of a poem by Alain Chartier written about 1424; and several poems probably belonging to the last part of the century, such as the *Flower and the Leaf*, the *Assembly of Ladies*, and *The Kingis Quair*. Courtly poetry is a genre that cannot be defined in a few words. A typical poem is often in the form of a dream vision, the dreamer finding himself in an idealized landscape. Here he might see a knight standing before a courtly assembly and making a "complaint" on the subject of love. Sometimes the landscape is inhabited by wondrous birds that debate about one subject or another, usually some aspect of courtly love. Sometimes the dreamer finds himself in a temple where he might see, depicted on the walls, various scenes relating to well-known love stories of antiquity. If the poem is not a dream poem, the narrator, after a sleepless night, often goes out into a flower-strewn meadow and sees unusual sights very similar to those in the dream poems. A courtly poem often carries along with it an elaborate allegory, with various personified abstractions appearing in almost every line and taking part in the meager action of the poem. Sometimes the gods and goddesses of antiquity are worked into the allegorical framework. The subject matter is usually serious, but seldom lugubrious and never morbid. The style of a courtly poem is decorative in language, restrained in the expression of feeling, and artificial in its total effect. It is thus in keeping with the sedateness of the subject matter and is well suited to a courtly, aristocratic audience.

Such is the exemplary courtly poem; but the genre was modified in various ways. Sometimes realistic, almost bourgeois elements ap-

[2] For a good discussion of courtly poetry see H. S. Bennett, *Chaucer and the Fifteenth Century* (Oxford, 1947), pp. 130-137.

pear in works that must still be labeled courtly. Something of this can already be seen in two of Chaucer's courtly poems, the *Parliament of Fowls* and the *House of Fame*. The grumbling discontent expressed by the lower orders of birds in the former poem and the lively discourse of the garrulous eagle in the latter are in striking contrast to the high-soaring thoughts couched in decorative language which one associates with the more conventional courtly poem. An even better example is the *Assembly of Gods,* a poem once attributed to Lydgate.[3] The work has all the trappings of a courtly poem — the dream vision, the painted walls, and an elaborate allegorical framework, with various gods and goddesses and personified abstractions. But at the same time it has realistic, lively, sometimes risqué dialogue and many proverbial lines.[4] These are some of the things one may also observe in Hoccleve's *Letter of Cupid.*

The *Letter* is an epistle from Cupid, the god of love, and it consists of a witty discussion of love and of the relationship between the sexes — always a favorite topic in courtly poetry. The work's real purpose, which becomes clearly manifest in the second half, is serious: namely, to defend women against the attacks of writers such as Jean de Meun. Various arguments against women are taken up and then refuted, one by one. The *Letter of Cupid,* however, is a bourgeois courtly poem, if I may use for a moment a paradoxical expression. The many realistic touches, sometimes in the form of bawdy direct discourse, make Hoccleve's work quite different from Lydgate's *Complaint of the Black Knight,* a courtly poem consisting also of a serious treatment of love and written in the same year that Hoccleve wrote the *Letter.*

A few examples will show what I mean. At one point in the original French poem Christine de Pisan introduces four lines of direct discourse in which a false lover slanders his friend's mistress:

> . . . "Je sçay bien de tes fais,
> Telle est t'amie et tu le jolis fais
> Pour sienne amour, mais pluseurs y ont part,
> Tu es receu quant un autre s'en part!"
>
> [vv. 127-130][5]

[3] Ed. Oscar Lovell Triggs, E.E.T.S., E.S., No. 69 (London, 1896).

[4] B. J. Whiting finds little proverbial material in Chaucer's dream poems — *Chaucer's Use of Proverbs,* Harvard Studies in Comparative Literature, XI (Cambridge, Mass., 1934), pp. 21 ff.

[5] All quotations from Christine's *Epistre au Dieu d'Amours* are taken from Maurice Roy's edition of the *Oeuvres Poëtiques de Christine de Pisan,* Société des Anciens Textes Français, No. 23, Pt. 2 (Paris, 1891), pp. 1-27.

Hoccleve adopts, reworks, and expands this idea, winding up with a colorful bit of masculine bawdy talk:

"Thou fisshist faire / shee þat hath thee fyrid,
Is fals / and inconstant / & hath no feith;
Shee for the rode of folk is so desyrid,
And as an hors fro day to day is hyrid,
That whan thow twynnest from hir conpaignie,
An othir comth / and blerid is thyn ye.

"Now prike on faste / & ryde thy iourneye;
whyl thow art ther / shee, behynde thy bak,
So liberal is / she can no wight withseye,
But qwikly of an othir take a snak;
For so the wommen faren, al the pak:
who-so hem trustith, hangid moot he be!
Ay they desiren chaunge & noueltee."
[Gollancz text, vv. 100-112]

The two stanzas are flippant in tone. Some of the words and phrases appear in such a context that one is invited to look for a deeper, and somewhat risqué, meaning. Since the noun "rode," the first of the images drawn from horsemanship, almost certainly has sexual connotations in this context, the temptation to find "bold bawdry" in the other images is justifiable. Indeed, one can read into the passage or between the lines about as much as he chooses. The whole thing is a good example of double entendre and one of Hoccleve's most striking early uses of direct discourse. In another bourgeois passage Hoccleve completely departs from his source and interpolates a stanza proverbial in tone and full of double entendre:

A foul vice is / of tonge to be light;
For who so mochil clappith / gabbith ofte.
The tonge of man, so swift is and so Wight,
þat whan it is areisid vp on lofte,
Reson it sueth / so slowly and softe
þat it him neuere ouertake may:
Lord, so the men been trusty at assay!
[vv. 141-147]

A coarse meaning is undoubtedly intended. One final example of Hoccleve's earthiness is an especially happy rendition of the original: in place of "femmes foles, / De pou d'onneur, males, maurenommées" (vv. 512-513) he writes "the foulest slutte / in al a town" (v. 237). These, then, are some of the individual touches Hoccleve gives his courtly poem that place it in a somewhat different category from works such as the *Book of the Duchess,* the Prologue to the *Legend of Good Women,* and the *Complaint of the Black Knight.*[6]

2. DIDACTIC POETRY

Hoccleve's magnum opus is the *Regement of Princes* (ca. 1412). It is a didactic poem, or, to be more specific, a manual of instruction for a prince. It consists of 5,463 lines, 24 of which are taken up by an envoy and 2,016 by a long prologue, which several earlier scholars considered the only interesting part of the poem. I shall be primarily concerned here with the 3,423 lines that come between the prologue and the envoy.

In the opening lines of the *Regement* proper, Hoccleve refers to three well-known medieval treatises, which he says he will use as source material. They are the *Secreta Secretorum,* which medieval writers attributed to Aristotle; Egidio Colonna's *De Regimine Principum*; and Jacobus de Cessolis' *Liber de Ludo Scacchorum.* Hoccleve's method of compilation, which he explains to Prince Hal, is to take important didactic passages widely scattered throughout the three Latin sources and to weave them together into a readable, entertaining whole (see vv. 2129-42). Friedrich Aster[7] has shown that Hoccleve actually does use the three sources indicated. The *Regement* is not, as many writers have thought and some still think, a translation of Egidio Colonna's *De Regimine Principum.* Interestingly, Hoccleve makes more use of the *Liber de Ludo Scacchorum* than either Egidio's treatise or the *Secreta Secretorum.* The error of assuming Hoccleve's work to be a translation of Egidio began in the fifteenth century[8] and has persisted, despite Aster, down to the present day.

The oldest of the three sources is the *Secreta Secretorum,* one of the most important works of medieval literature. It seems to have been written originally in Syriac during the eighth century, perhaps by a physician, and translated shortly thereafter into Arabic. It pretends to be a manual of instruction written by Aristotle for Alexander the Great. The definitive study of the work's history is by

[6] For a thorough discussion of the *Letter* in relation to its source, see Chapter IV.

[7] *Das Verhältniss des altenglischen Gedichtes "De Regimine Principum" von Thomas Hoccleve zu seinen Quellen nebst einer Einleitung über Leben und Werke des Dichters* (diss. Leipzig, 1888).

[8] See Allan H. Gilbert, "Notes on the Influence of the *Secretum Secretorum,*" *Speculum,* III (1928), 94, n. 1.

Robert Steele,[9] who distinguishes between a Western and an Eastern Arabic Form. The former, translated into Latin in the early twelfth century by Johannes Hispalensis (or Hispaniensis), exists in many manuscripts and in one printed text. The longer Eastern Form was translated into Latin in the first half of the thirteenth century. In succeeding years this version was revised and reworked by several writers, including Roger Bacon. Various Latin versions appeared in the early years of printing until finally, in 1501, a text was published that has been copied in all subsequent editions. This was an edition by Alexander Achillini, a physician and jurist of Bologna. The parts of the *Secreta* printed by Aster are from a 1516 Achillini text.

The popularity of the *Secreta Secretorum* during the Middle Ages is shown by the widespread number of manuscripts in several different languages. The *Secreta* also influenced other manuals of instruction for princes, including the *De Administratione Principum* and *De Eruditio Principum* of Pope Innocent III (ob. 1216); the *De Instructione Principis* of Giraldus Cambrensis (ob. ca. 1220); the *De Regimine Principum* of Vincent of Beauvais (composed ca. 1263); the *De Regimine Principum* of St. Guillaume Peraldi (ob. 1275); and the *De Regimine Principum* of Egidio Colonna (ob. 1316).[10] The list is far from complete. In English, Gower made use of material from the *Secreta* in the *Confessio Amantis,* Book VII. There are also three fifteenth-century prose versions, one of which possibly antedates Hoccleve's *Regement.*[11] Lydgate and Benedict Burgh did the first separate translation in verse.[12]

In translating and paraphrasing parts of the *Secreta* in his *Regement,* Hoccleve made use of one of the most popular didactic treatises of the Middle Ages. The *Regement* shows his dependence on well-known traditional genres. The passages he took directly from the Latin have been pointed out by Aster and by Allan H. Gilbert (see n. 8 above). The *Regement of Princes* is one of the earliest occurrences of the *Secreta Secretorum* in English.

Hoccleve's second principal source is the *De Regimine Principum*

[9] Ed. Roger Bacon's *Secretum Secretorum, Opera Hactenus Inedita Rogeri Baconi,* Fasc. V (Oxford, 1920), pp. vii-lxiv.

[10] See Steele, p. ix; and Oliver A. Beckerlegge's edition of *Le Secré de Secrez* by Pierre D'Abernun of Fetcham, Anglo-Norman Text Society, No. 5 (Oxford, 1944), pp. xxv-xxvi.

[11] *Three Prose Versions of the Secreta Secretorum,* ed. Robert Steele, E.E.T.S., E.S., No. 74 (London, 1898).

[12] Lydgate and Burgh's *Secrees of Old Philisoffres,* ed. Robert Steele, E.E.T.S., E.S., No. 66 (London, 1894).

of Egidio Colonna (ca. 1247-1316),[13] who compiled the treatise at the request of King Philip III for the instruction of the prince, Philip the Fair. Its purpose is to give princes all the instruction needed for them to govern successfully themselves, their household, and their state. The work is divided accordingly into three books, each of which is subdivided into three parts except the first, which has four parts. Aster has shown that all the material used by Hoccleve appears in the first and second parts of Book I. Egidio's *De Regimine Principum* was well known throughout the later Middle Ages and was printed several times during the fifteenth, sixteenth, and early seventeenth centuries. Hoccleve's use of it, along with his use of the *Secreta,* is a clear example of his dependence on traditional genres. The excerpts from Egidio printed by Aster are from a 1556 edition. Translations of Egidio's Latin have been published in French, German, Italian, and Spanish — but not in English. John Trevisa translated the work into English about 1390, but his translation exists only in a single manuscript.[14] Hoccleve's use of selected passages from Egidio's *De Regimine Principum* is the only well-known occurrence of the work in English.

The third principal source of the *Regement* — and the one Hoccleve used most extensively — is Jacobus de Cessolis' *Liber de Ludo Scacchorum.*[15] A Dominican friar at Rheims, Jacobus flourished around 1300. The stories and anecdotes he relates make the *Ludus Scacchorum* a manual of sugar-coated instruction, not only for princes but for everyone, all social strata being represented by the various chessmen. The stories are taken from a number of different sources — St. Jerome, Valerius Maximus, Seneca — some of whom

[13] The best source of information on Egidio Colonna is Félix Lajard's "Gilles de Rome, Religieux Augustin, Théologien," included in *Histoire Littéraire de la France,* XXX (Paris, 1888), 421-566. Egidio Colonna (or Aegidius Columna or Aegidius Romanus) should not be confused with Guido delle Colonne. Furnivall makes this mistake.

[14] Bodl. Libr. MS. Digby 233. Aaron J. Perry was preparing an edition, "but he died in 1952 with his work still unfinished" — David C. Fowler, "New Light on John Trevisa," *Traditio,* XVIII (1962), 316, n. 108. Mrs. Perry turned over her husband's manuscripts to Professor Fowler so that the project might be completed. Dr. Kenneth C. Conroy has prepared a glossary of Trevisa's translation of the *De Regimine Principum* as a Ph.D. dissertation (University of Washington, Seattle, 1964). At the present time Dr. Conroy is preparing the complete text for publication.

[15] For a good study of Jacobus de Cessolis with useful lists of MSS and early printed editions of the *Liber de Ludo Scacchorum,* see Anton Schmid, *Literatur des Schachspiels* (Vienna, 1847), pp. 9-43.

Jacobus mentions. Judging from the large number of manuscripts and early printed editions, one can say that the *Liber de Ludo Scacchorum* was quite popular. But despite the existence of manuscript versions in vernacular languages such as German, French, Dutch, and Italian, the work was not known in its entirety in English until Caxton published his translation from the French in 1475. Hoccleve's borrowings are the only occurrence of the *Ludus Scacchorum* in English before Caxton. Some of the stories, however, in versions other than those of Jacobus, can be found in the seventh book of the *Confessio Amantis*.[16] Others bear a strong resemblance to stories in the *Gesta Romanorum*.

Using an edition of 1505 Aster gives fifty-two instances in which Hoccleve has either translated or paraphrased material from the *Liber de Ludo Scacchorum*. The anecdotes vary considerably in length. Some are more in the realm of allusions than anecdotes and amount to only a few lines; others add up to thirty or forty lines in Hoccleve's poem; and one, the Story of John of Canace, extends to 174 lines. The latter instance, however, is an exception, for it is about twice the length of the parallel material in Jacobus. It is tempting to attribute the added details to Hoccleve's own invention; but one must in all fairness recognize that Hoccleve may have translated from a manuscript of the *Liber* which differed from the printed edition used by Aster, or he may have seen or possessed a version of the story which differed from that of Jacobus. The various stories and anecdotes drawn by Hoccleve from the *Liber de Ludo Scacchorum* add up to approximately 1,000 lines — that is, roughly 30 per cent of the *Regement* proper.

Hoccleve refers to his three principal sources, as I have already indicated, in the opening lines of the *Regement* proper — a section that Furnivall calls the "Proem." He also refers here to Chaucer (vv. 2077-2107), whom he praises highly, lamenting his death with such a convincing emotional display that many writers have argued that there must have been a close personal relationship between Hoccleve and Chaucer. It is possible, however, that the passage is largely conventional (see Chapter VI, Section 2). The "Proem" concludes with a few lines of conventional self-deprecation.

Furnivall conveniently divides the *Regement* into fifteen sections according to the different virtues that Hoccleve believes are desirable

[16] See G. C. Macaulay's notes to his edition of *The English Works of John Gower*, Pt. 2, E.E.T.S., E.S., No. 82 (London, 1901).

in a monarch. The sections vary in length and importance. The first (which Furnivall calls "On the Dignity of a King") consists of only four stanzas. Hoccleve urges Prince Henry to learn well the dignity that befits a king, and he gives a short anecdote of a king who once told his crown that it cost him his ease and that anyone who fully understood the dangers and responsibility in wearing it would never want to be crowned. The second section consists of a long discussion of the necessity of a king's keeping his coronation oaths and of the importance of truth and cautious speech. One of the *exempla* Hoccleve relates is the story of Marcus Regulus, a Roman soldier who preferred to die in a Carthaginian prison rather than break an oath. Alluding to the contemporary scene, he writes that there are few men of his day as noble as Marcus Regulus. He urges Prince Henry to keep all promises that he makes. Finally, he advises the prince to beware of talking too much and to be particularly cautious in everything he says publicly. The third section is devoted to the subject of justice. Here, as in most sections, Hoccleve defines and discusses the virtue he believes a monarch should have and then adds several illustrative anecdotes. In the fourth section he stresses the importance of a monarch's observing the laws of the land, and during the course of the discussion he refers to the situation in England. Having observed that wealthy, influential people often assemble in arms and refuse to submit themselves to judges, he fears that law is nonexistent in England. In the fifth section he turns to the subject of pity. He tells the well-known story of the workman who devised an instrument of death in the form of a brazen bull. The pitiless workman lost his own life when his equally pitiless master decided to test the instrument's efficiency on its inventor. Thus his attempt to flatter his lord ended in failure. Hoccleve then digresses on the evils of flattery, a conventional topic with which he had concerned himself ten years earlier in *La Male Regle*. Returning to the subject of pity, he advises the prince to show pity toward all his people — to all, that is, except murderers, who should always be executed for the sake of order in the realm.

The following sections are on mercy, patience (and humility), chastity (and abstinence), magnanimity, and covetousness, each containing one or more illustrative anecdotes. In the eleventh section Hoccleve discusses liberality and prodigality. He tells the story of John of Canace, a wealthy man who bestowed all his riches on his two daughters and then, like Shakespeare's Lear, regretted he had done so because of their unkindness toward him. Hoccleve tells the prince that he, like John of Canace, spent money foolishly in past years and that now he finds himself in straitened circumstances. He urges the prince to help him obtain his overdue annuity. The intrusion of the personal element is one of the individual touches Hoccleve gives to his *Regement.* In the next section he discusses avarice and suggests that the prince freely bestow gifts on people who deserve them, the implication being that he himself is one of the most deserving of all the prince's subjects. The thirteenth section is on the importance of prudence. Hoccleve tells the prince that if he grants an annuity to a man, he should pay it regularly. The implication, of course, is that his own annuity is long overdue. In the next section he stresses the importance of counsel. A monarch must guard himself against flatterers, avaricious courtiers, and impetuous, youthful advisers. Urging Prince Henry not to listen to counsel on holy days, he suddenly recalls that Chaucer had written on a similar subject (perhaps the passage on counsel in the *Tale of Melibee*) and digresses on the excellence of his late master. At this point some manuscripts contain a miniature portrait of Chaucer (see Chapter VI, Section 1). Hoccleve believes that the portrait will cause people to think about Chaucer, just as the images in churches lead worshippers to think on God and the saints.

The fifteenth and last section is on the subject of peace. Hoccleve talks at some length on the ways of achieving peace in the home, and he concludes that it can come about only if men recognize the superiority of women and willingly submit themselves to their wives' better judgment. Here, as in other poems, he reveals marked feminist sympathies. He then turns from the question of peace in the home to peace within the country. He observes that civil wars have claimed the lives of thousands of Englishmen. He believes that discord is often caused by flatterers and avaricious courtiers. He deplores the existence of internal conflict in France and looks forward to the day when the Christian princes of England and France will make peace with one another. Interestingly, he foresees an end to all strife in the marriage of Prince Hal and Princess Katherine of France. In conclusion, he exhorts England and France to unite in arms and make war on the enemies of Christ.

Hoccleve's *Regement* stands at the beginning of a succession of English manuals of instruction for a prince. I have already mentioned Lydgate and Burgh's verse translation of the *Secreta Secre-*

torum (ca. 1450). George Ashby's *Active Policy of a Prince* (ca. 1470) contains much advice that could be found in one form or another in the *Secreta.* His verse translation of the *Dicta & Opiniones Diversorum Philosophorum* belongs also to the *regement* tradition.[17] The popularity of the genre did not come to an end in the fifteenth century. In 1511 Pynson printed Lydgate and Burgh's translation of the *Secreta* under the title *The Gouernaunce of Kynges and Prynces.*[18] Two famous sixteenth-century courtesy books — Elyot's *Boke Named the Gouernour* and Hoby's *Book of the Courtier* — represent a further evolution of the genre. In addition to these titles there are several works which do not purport to be manuals of instruction but which actually contain a great deal of advice to princes. One of these is Lydgate's *Siege of Thebes,* another his *Fall of Princes.*

Clearly Hoccleve's *Regement of Princes* belongs to a well-established, traditional genre. But unlike other *regements* his contains a long prologue full of autobiographical allusions and references to important social questions of the times. And in the *Regement* proper the didactic element is made entertaining, partly through the poet's digressions and partly through his attempt to make the work of current interest by commenting on contemporary social problems and on the political situation in France. In addition, Hoccleve shows originality in his handling of direct discourse, often expanding parallel material in his source and heightening its dramatic intensity (see Chapter IV). Also significant is his interspersing purely didactic material with stories and anecdotes, many of which had never before appeared in English. There are more than forty manuscripts of the *Regement of Princes.* The simple fact that it is in English may account for much of its popularity in the fifteenth century.

To sum up, Hoccleve's *Regement* is one of the earliest English works to make use of the *Secreta Secretorum.* Moreover, with the exception of Trevisa's translation, which seems never to have been well known, it is the first (indeed the only) English manual of instruction to make use of Egidio Colonna's *De Regimine Principum.* It is also the earliest occurrence in English of stories from the *Liber de Ludo Scacchorum* and was not superseded until Caxton pub-

[17] *George Ashby's Poems,* ed. Mary Bateson, E.E.T.S., E.S., No. 76 (London, 1899).

[18] Reproduced in facsimile, with an introduction by DeWitt T. Starnes (Gainesville, Fla., 1957).

lished his complete translation in 1475. It is virtually the first full-fledged English manual of instruction for a prince. Because of the great interest in works of this kind during the Middle Ages — an interest proved by the large number of Latin treatises and the existence of scores of manuscripts in both Latin and the vernacular — Hoccleve's *Regement of Princes* could hardly have failed to please a fifteenth-century English public. If modern critics find his work dull, they would undoubtedly be bored by other manuals of instruction for a prince. The genre has long been out of fashion.

3. POLITICAL POEMS

The *Regement of Princes* can best be classified as a didactic poem, but the passages on the social problems in England and the political situation in France bring it also into the realm of political verse. In addition, Hoccleve wrote a number of separate political poems. His best-known work of this kind is the *Address to Sir John Oldcastle,* in which he inveighs against the knight's heretical opinions and urges him to return to the true faith. At the time Hoccleve wrote the *Address* (1415), Oldcastle had already been once imprisoned for heresy; but he had escaped, and was hiding in Wales with a band of his fellow Lollards. Occasionally the heretics would raid defenseless villages for plunder. Thus what was first a religious dispute was now a serious political problem.

Hoccleve's poem consists of 521 lines of eight-line pentameter stanzas and divides into two almost equal parts. In the first part the poet addresses Sir John in a long apostrophe, telling him that he is "fro Crystes feith twynned & goon" (v. 8). He exhorts Oldcastle to quench his pride, obey Holy Church, and repent. Two aspects of the knight's heresy are his objection to confession and his refusal to obey prelates. Hoccleve presents the conventional rebuttal that even if a priest is wicked, one can still obey his teaching and go to confession. He urges Oldcastle not to stir up arguments about the faith. He deplores that even some women of his day argue about Holy Writ (perhaps a reference to Margery Kempe), and he advises them to sit at home at the spinning wheel and "kakele of sumwhat elles" (v. 148). He tells Oldcastle that since their forefathers never questioned the teaching of the Church, neither should they. Just as a man defends his inheritance from robbers, so their forefathers held Christ's faith against the onslaught of heretical doctrines. A person who will not defend his inheritance, whether it be property or religion, is a coward. Hoccleve advises Oldcastle to read books of chivalry such as *Lancelot du Lake* and the *Siege of Thebes* or perhaps books from the Bible such as Judges, Kings, and Joshua, but to leave arguments about Holy Writ to the Church. The Roman emperor Constantine obeyed the teaching of the Church, and so also does King Henry V — both of whom Sir John should try to emulate. In the final stanza of Part I, Hoccleve calls on God to inspire Oldcastle with divine grace and to forgive him for his heresy.

The second part consists mostly of a long apostrophe to the wicked heretics who have led Sir John astray. Hoccleve considers several opinions associated with the Lollard movement (such as the objections to images and to the holding of property by the Church) and refutes them by appealing to the teaching of Holy Church. He notes that Christ's disciples faced death boldly, whereas the Lollards hide in dark corners (i.e., in Wales) and come out into the open only to slay helpless, unprotected people. In the last three stanzas Hoccleve calls once more on Oldcastle to renounce his ways, humble himself before the king, and return to the true faith.

There are other pieces, anonymous, relating to the religious disputes of the times. One poem against the Lollards has been printed several times, most recently by Rossell Hope Robbins in *Historical Poems of the XIVth and XVth Centuries* (New York, 1959), pp. 152-157. It is a vicious attack on Lollardry with abusive allusions to Sir John Oldcastle. Thus it differs from Hoccleve's *Address,* because Hoccleve, although highly critical of heretical doctrines, maintains respect for the knight and seriously urges him to change his views.[19] Other political poems by Hoccleve are the *Balade to King Henry V on His Accession to the Throne,* the *Two Balades to Henry V and the Knights of the Garter,* and the *Balade After King Richard II's Bones Were Brought to Westminster.* Like Lydgate's work in the same vein, Hoccleve's verse is official rather than poetical. Except for his attitude toward heresy, which is apparently sincere, the personal element is lacking. Hoccleve has no popular battle ballads, no war poems like those of Lawrence Minot, and no poems in sympathy with some popular struggle. His political verse, like that of Lydgate and Gower, was designed for court circles. It is of interest today largely for historical reasons: that is, it is a good primary

[19] For a more complete discussion of the attitude of Hoccleve and other fifteenth-century writers toward the Lollards, see Section 7 below.

source of information on various aspects of the political scene in the early fifteenth century. Not much more can be expected of medieval political verse.

4. BEGGING POEMS

Hoccleve wrote several short, conventional poems of solicitation for money, all of which apparently stem from Chaucer's *Complaint to His Purse.* Sometimes he sounds a plaintive note, as in the *Balade to My Lord the Chancellor* and the *Balade to King Henry V for Money.* At other times he is good-humored and colloquial, as in the *Balade to My Maister Carpenter.* And occasionally he is witty, as in the two poems of solicitation addressed to Henry Somer. The latter's name offers Hoccleve an excellent opportunity to pun:

> Now, syn þat sonne may so moche auaill,
> And moost with Somer is his soiournynge,
> That sesoun bounteuous we wole assaill.
>
> [*Balade and Roundel to Mr. Henry Somer,* vv. 5-8]

None of Hoccleve's witty begging poems, however, is so cleverly wrought as Lydgate's *Letter to Gloucester,* with its subtle metaphorical conceits and alchemic terminology. But Lydgate did not write so many begging poems as did Hoccleve. Interestingly, Hoccleve's pieces make up a high percentage of the English poems belonging to the genre. Moreover, his requests for money are not confined to the short poems of solicitation. At the end of *La Male Regle,* for example, he asks the god Health to tell Lord Fourneval, the treasurer, to pay him his overdue annuity. In the *Regement of Princes* he also complains about his lack of funds, obviously with the hope that Prince Henry will come to his assistance. In addition, there are cases where one suspects that Hoccleve is writing with an ulterior motive. Two short poems in which he commends himself to noble personages — the *Balade to My Gracious Lord of York* and the *Balade to the Duke of Bedford* — can be looked upon as poems of indirect solicitation.

It is difficult to say just how much of the personal element Hoccleve's complaints to his empty purse contain. The *short* pieces, several of which are virelays, obviously belong to a traditional genre and therefore do not necessarily reflect the poet's personal feelings. We are left, then, with the passages of solicitation in the longer poems. The urgent tone Hoccleve sounds certainly gives the impression of sincerity. Yet, as was pointed out in the last chapter, the governmental records indicate that he was fairly well off financially, at least in comparison with other white-collar workers.

5. RELIGIOUS VERSE

Religious lyrics form an important group of poems within the Hoccleve canon, one of which, the *Mother of God,* was once thought to be the work of Chaucer. In discussing medieval religious poetry one should bear several things in mind.[20] First, most of it is highly conventional; that is, the same images, descriptive epithets, and forms of expression occur in works of many different writers. Medieval religious verse seldom reveals an emotional experience peculiar to an individual poet. Much of it was written to fulfill certain practical purposes in the divine service and therefore has the character of applied art. Moreover, religious poetry, conventional though it is, did not remain static throughout the Middle Ages but was modified from time to time, as can be seen in the Marian lyrics.[21] In early medieval Latin hymns Mary was thought of as the holy Mother of God, the pure, everlasting Virgin, the helper in God's salvation of mankind. Later, partly through the influence of the sermons and devotional poetry of the thirteenth-century Franciscans, the concept of Mary changed. She became humanized. Another interesting development is that courtly diction from the love poetry of the French tradition became mixed up with religious poetry, the result being that many English hymns to the Virgin sound like a lover's complaint to his mistress. The fifteenth century presents still more problems. Because some poets reveled in aureate diction, rhetoric, and bombastic repetition, many of the Marian lyrics, especially those of Lydgate, are highly affected in style and completely devoid of any genuine, personal religious feeling. This is the "new religious style" of the fifteenth century — "a style characterized by majesty, heroic dignity, and solemn grandeur." The concept of Mary changes along with the change in style. She becomes now "the queen of heaven, the image radiating mercy, enshrined in mystical ornamen-

[20] In the following discussion I am much indebted to Professor Walter F. Schirmer's chapter on "Lydgate's Religious Verse" in his *John Lydgate: A Study in the Culture of the XVth Century,* trans. Ann E. Keep (Berkeley and Los Angeles, 1961), pp. 173-197.

[21] The most complete study of the English Marian lyrics is Theodor Wolpers' "Geschichte der Englischen Marienlyrik im Mittelalter" (unpubl. diss. Bonn, 1949). See the abridged version (to which I am indebted) in *Anglia,* LXIX (1950), 3-88.

tation."[22] The religious verse of Lydgate is clearly a manifestation of the new religious style. Hoccleve's religious verse, however, is quite different. The following discussion attempts to show that Hoccleve did not adopt the new religious style of the fifteenth century.

The *Mother of God* will serve as a convenient point of departure. It resembles Chaucer's *ABC* very closely in subject matter and style. Both are prayers to the Virgin, and in both the poetic diction is very similar:

Mother of God	*An ABC*
Benigne confort of vs wrecches alle [v. 15]	Queen of comfort . . . [v. 121]
O welle of pitee / vn-to thee I calle [v. 17]	Who, but thiself, that art of pitee welle [v. 126]
Ful of swetnesse . . . [v. 18]	But ful of swetnesse and of merci evere [v. 51]
O blessid lady / the cleer light of day [v. 29]	And therfore, ladi bright, thou for us praye [v. 62]
Temple of our lord / and roote of all goodnesse [v. 30]	Temple devout, ther God hath his woninge [v. 145]
Swich an aduocatrice, who can dyuyne [v. 40]	Ne advocat noon that wole and dar so preye [v. 102]
Mene for vs, flour of humilitee [v. 44]	Who shal unto thi Sone my mene bee [v. 125]
	. . . O freshe flour [v. 159]
Lady pitous, virgyne wemmelees [v. 93]	Was signe of thin unwemmed maidenhede [v. 91]
To wasshe away our cloudeful offense [v. 109]	To wasshe sinful soule out of his gilt [v. 178]
And of my soule / wasshe away the sore [v. 140]	

These illustrative examples do not prove necessarily that Hoccleve borrowed from Chaucer. They are conventional forms of expression that occur in many medieval religious lyrics. The piety expressed seems more the characteristic expression of piety of the times than evidence of personal religious feeling. Observe Hoccleve's diction in the following stanza from the *Mother of God* and in a stanza from another of his prayers to the Virgin:

O blessid lady / the cleer light of day!
Temple of our lord / and roote of al goodnesse!

[22] Schirmer, p. 197.

þat by prayere wypest cleene away
The filthes of our synful wikkidnesse,
Thyn hand foorth putte / & helpe my distresse,
And fro temptacioun deliure me
Of wikkid thoght / thurgh thy benignitee . . .
[*Mother of God,* vv. 29-35]

Worsshipful maiden to the world / Marie,
Modir moost louynge vn-to al man-kynde,
Lady to whom al synful peple crie
In hir distresse / haue vs in thy mynde!
Thurgh thy benigne pitee, vs vnbynde
Of our giltes / þat, in thy sones birthe,
To al the world broghtest the ioie & mirthe!
[*Ad Beatam Virginem,* vv. 1-7]

Both examples are obviously conventional; that is, Hoccleve has employed metaphorical conceits and religious phraseology which he most certainly did not invent.

Lydgate's religious verse is also conventional. Yet the most cursory comparison of the foregoing illustrations with passages from Lydgate reveals marked differences. Here, for example, are three stanzas selected at random from Lydgate's Marian hymns:[23]

Celestial cipresse set vpon Syon,
Hiest Cidre of perfit holynesse,
Charboncle of charite and grene emerawd ston,
Hool & vnbroken by virgynal clennesse,
O Saphir loup al swellyng to represse,
Off cankred sores & venymous feloun,
In gostly woundes be ther gouerneresse
To thy .v. Ioies þat haue deuocioun.
[*To Mary, the Queen of Heaven,* vv. 9-16]

Hayle luminary & benigne lanterne,
Of Ierusalem the holy ordres nyne,
As quene of quenes laudacion eterne
They yeue to thee, O excellente virgyne!
Eclypsyd I am, for to determyne
Thy superexcellence of Cantica canticorum,
The aureat beames do nat in me shyne,
Aue regina celorum!
[*Ave Regina Celorum,* vv. 1-8]

O thow ioyfull lyght! eternall ye shyne,
In glory with Laureat coronall,
Descendyd from Dauid, worthyest on lyne,

[23] *The Minor Poems of John Lydgate,* ed. Henry Noble MacCracken, Pt. 1, E.E.T.S., E.S., No. 107 (London, 1911 [for 1910]).

Modyr to your soueraynes, & Lord imperyall;
Elect to grace from synne oryginall,
Floure of clennes and pure virginite!
Sith ye be mayde and moder in speciall,
Regina celi, letare!

[*Regina Celi Letare,* vv. 1-8]

The stanzas are excellent illustrations of Lydgate's "invocatory" style; the language is decorative, pretentious, and sonorously verbose. Mary is clearly a supernal essence, enthroned in glory far above creatures of flesh and blood. The stanzas from Hoccleve, in contrast, which are pitched in a lower key, present a different conception of the Virgin. Hoccleve does not emphasize her celestial brightness and splendor so much as he does her willingness to save mankind from the corruption of sin. To put it differently, there is a definite contact between the sinner and the Virgin not to be found in Lydgate's religious verse. Hoccleve implores her to unbind him from his guilts, to put forth her hand and help him in his distress. Lydgate sings her praises but does not seek, or even imagine, a closer relationship. My observations about Hoccleve's Marian hymns apply also to his prayers *Ad Patrem, Ad Filium,* and *Ad Spiritum Sanctum.* The poems are conventional and probably devoid of personal feeling; but Hoccleve's conception of the Deity implies a closer relationship between man and his Maker than one can find in Lydgate's religious verse. This is particularly noticeable in the prayer *Ad Filium,* in which Hoccleve thinks of Jesus primarily in human terms. The first two stanzas are representative of the entire poem:

O blessid chyld Iesu / what haast thow do,
þat for vs shuldist souffre swich Iewyse?
Louynge chyld / what stired thee ther-to,
That thow woldest be treted in swich wyse?
what causid thee to take þat empryse?
what was thy gilt, and thyn offense, I preye,
And cause of deeth / and dampnyng eek, I seye?

I am the wownde of al thy greuance;
I am the cause of thyn occisioun,
And of thy deeth / dessert / of thy vengeance
I am also verray flagicioun;
I causid thee thy greuous passioun;
Of thy torment I am solicitour,
Thow goddes sone / our Lord & Sauueour!

Lydgate's approach is altogether different: he would not address the Deity in such an intimate fashion. All the illustrations in the foregoing discussion point out the essential differences between the religious poetry of Hoccleve and that of Lydgate. Hoccleve's lyrics cannot be considered examples of the new religious style.

One of Hoccleve's Marian lyrics is a *planctus Mariae,* or a lament of the Virgin at the scene of the crucifixion — a well-established genre in the Middle Ages. She speaks in some poems while Christ is still nailed upon the cross and in others while she is holding His body in her arms. The latter idea is represented in sculpture by Michelangelo's *Pietà,* the former in poetry by Hoccleve's *Compleynte of the Virgin Before the Cross.*

The poem is made up of a series of apostrophes. In the first ten stanzas Mary calls on God; the Holy Ghost; the angel Gabriel; Elizabeth, mother of John the Baptist; the woman who once said to Christ, "Blessed is the womb that bare thee, and the paps which thou hast sucked" (Luke xi:27); Simeon (Luke ii:25-35); and her parents, Joachim and Anne. She emphasizes the contrast between her former joy and her present sorrow, and she feels that those whom she is apostrophizing have forsaken her. In the next seven stanzas she addresses Christ in intimate terms, telling Him how much she is grieved to see Him suffer. One remarkable human touch in Hoccleve's depiction of Mary is the concern she shows about her son's being crucified along with two common thieves. In stanza xviii she calls on death to slay her too, and in stanzas xix-xxiii she addresses the moon, the stars, the firmament, the sun, and the earth. She feels that the earth and the heavens themselves have turned against her son in His adversity. In the remaining stanzas she calls once more on Christ; then on the apostle John, the angels, and even herself; and finally on the sons of Adam, whom she urges to draw near and show their love for one who died for their sins.

In this work Hoccleve's conception of the Virgin as a human being is best illustrated. The following stanza is typical of the poem's intimate diction:

> O blessid sone / on thee wole I out throwe
> My salte teeres / for oonly on thee
> My look is set / o thynke / how many a throwe
> Thow in myn armes lay / and on my knee
> Thow sat / & haddist many a kus of me.
> Eeek thee, to sowke, on my breestes yaf y,
> Thee norisshyng faire & tendrely.
>
> [vv. 71-77]

The Mary depicted here is completely different from Lydgate's awesome queen of heaven. Lydgate has only one *planctus* — *Quis Dabit Meo Capiti Fontem Lacrimarum* — but even here he consciously strives for a grandiose effect. He does not depict a human mother grieving for the death of her human son. Hoccleve's *Compleynte of the Virgin* is much closer in spirit to an anonymous *planctus* included by Carleton Brown in *Religious Lyrics of the XVth Century* (Oxford, 1939), pp. 13-16. Here also the human element is predominant. Brown believes that "in imaginative description and human pathos" this *planctus* and the one immediately preceding it in the collection "surpass all earlier treatments of this theme" (p. xxi). Like the anonymous *planctus,* Hoccleve's work is a conspicuous example of the depiction of the Blessed Virgin in human terms. But the human element notwithstanding, it would be unwise to see in the poem any indication of Hoccleve's personal feelings toward his subject. All one can say with certainty is that the *Compleynte* belongs to a traditional medieval genre, the *planctus Mariae,* and more specifically to a group of conventional poems within the genre that emphasize the human attributes of the Virgin.[24]

In addition to the various types of religious poetry just discussed, Hoccleve has one poem belonging to another distinct genre — his *Legend of the Virgin and Her Sleeveless Garment.*[25] The story concerns a monk who says fifty *Ave Marias* each day in the chapel of his abbey. One day the Blessed Virgin appears before him in a sleeveless garment. She tells him to treble the number of his *Ave Marias* and to add a *Pater noster* to every tenth *Ave.* If he will do her commandment, she promises to come to him again on the next holy day. The monk does as she says. On the next holy day she appears before him again, this time freshly arrayed in complete dress. In speaking with him she predicts that he will soon become an abbot and after seven years leave this life to join her in heaven. All that she says comes to pass. In the final stanza Hoccleve recommends that his readers say the proper number of *Aves* to the Virgin so that they may stand in her grace.

[24] Hoccleve's *Compleynte* is based on a French *planctus* by Deguileville included in his *Pèlerinage de l'Ame.* For a brief comparison of the two poems, see Furnivall's forewords to his edition of the *Regement of Princes,* p. x.

[25] For the following remarks I am indebted to Beverly Boyd, "Hoccleve's Miracle of the Virgin," *University of Texas Studies in English,* XXXV (1956), 116-122.

The poem belongs to a group of legends revolving about the reciting of *Ave Marias*. It was a custom in medieval times to recite *Ave Marias* in multiples of 150, and since this is the exact number of psalms in the Psalter, the custom was known as Our Lady's Psalter. An older poetical version of the same legend can be found in Digby MS. 86 and in the Auchinleck manuscript. The latter manuscript is one which Hoccleve may have had the opportunity to read.[26] The Digby-Auchinleck poem and Hoccleve's work are apparently the only two versions in English of the legend of the Virgin and her sleeveless garment. In fact, they are the only English examples, so far as I know, of legends about Our Lady's Psalter.

Hoccleve wrote no metrical saints' legends, no passion poems, no verses to accompany religious processions, no sermons in rhyme, and no poems in the form of words of admonition spoken by Jesus from the cross. Thus, as a writer of religious verse, he does not approach Lydgate in versatility. But despite gaps in certain traditional genres his metrical *Ars Moriendi* — something Lydgate never attempted — assures him of an important place in the history of fifteenth-century religious poetry.

Literature of the *Ars Moriendi* variety was extremely popular throughout the Middle Ages. Many different versions exist, all of them related in one way or another. The problem of establishing exactly how they relate is difficult,[27] but perhaps all derive ultimately from the second chapter of the second book of Heinrich Suso's *Horologium Sapientiae* (1334). This has been shown by Kurtz to be the original of Hoccleve's *Lerne to Dye* as well as of a number of fifteenth-century Middle English prose versions.[28] Since Hoccleve's *Lerne to Dye* belongs to the early 1420's, it is certainly an early, if not the very first, treatment of the *Ars Moriendi* in English. It is the only fifteenth-century poetical version.

In structure the poem is like a frame story. The beginning and the end consist of conversations between a disciple and his mentor, Eternal Wisdom. The middle part, or the picture itself, consists of a lament of a young man on his deathbed together with his admonitory remarks to the disciple, who questions him about his fear of death. In the opening stanzas, largely didactic, the disciple asks

[26] *Ibid.*, p. 120.

[27] See Frances M. M. Comper, ed., *The Book of the Craft of Dying and Other Early English Tracts Concerning Death* (London, 1917), p. 49.

[28] Benjamin P. Kurtz, "The Source of Occleve's *Lerne to Dye*," *MLN*, XXXVIII (1923), 337-340.

Eternal Wisdom to reveal to him her treasure of wisdom. She tells him that she will teach him the art of learning how to die — a difficult art, but most important. She then shows him a vision of a young man dying, at whose bedside is a figure resembling the disciple himself. What follows is the heart of the poem. The young man is afflicted with a painful, mortal disease, and he is terrified at the approach of death:

"O deeth, o deeth, greet is thy crueltee!
Thyn office al to sodeynly doost thow.
Is ther no grace? lakkist thow pitee?
Spare my youthe / of age rype ynow
To dye / am y nat yit / spare me now!"
[vv. 141-145]

The disciple asks him why he thinks death should spare him when even the prophets of old had to die. He replies that he is grieved, not because he must die, but because he has led a sinful life and must suffer the consequences. When the disciple advises him to turn to God and repent, he replies that it is now too late. His understanding is so damaged by the ravages of illness that he could not possibly know whether or not his penance were sincere. He regrets that he did not turn to God when there was still time. The disciple then asks for advice on how he might avoid the same fate. The young man urges him to confess his sins, make amends for them, and behave as if he were to die that very day. He says that the disciple should hereafter think on his grievous affliction and remember how miserable one is who is not ready to die. Suddenly the agony of the dying man becomes even more pronounced. He sees a vision of the suffering souls in purgatory which he quickly relates to the disciple. He dies. In the last part of the poem (the frame again) the disciple, greatly moved at the young man's death, decides to give up the vanities of the world and prays for punishment in this life instead of the life hereafter. Eternal Wisdom bids him to make amends for his sinful past life while there is still time and to commit himself to God's mercy. She tells him that the fear of God is the beginning of wisdom. Finally, she says that if he thinks just on the death of those whom he has known in his short lifetime, he will fully realize the vital importance of preparing himself for death.

The relation of the *Lerne to Dye* to its Latin source has been studied in great detail by Kurtz.[29] Although Hoccleve did not trans-

[29] "The Relation of Occleve's *Lerne to Dye* to Its Source, *PMLA*, XL (1925), 252-275.

late the entire chapter from the *Horologium,* his poem is slightly more than twice as long. The expansion has been brought about by free translation and original additions. In most cases, Kurtz believes, Hoccleve has amplified the original simply to overcome the exigencies of the metrical pattern. While thoroughly convinced that Hoccleve is a bad poet, Kurtz has to admit, nevertheless, that some of the additional material, especially in the didactic portions, is actually more convincing from a dramatic standpoint (practically the whole poem is in direct discourse), and therefore decidedly more effective, than the original Latin. Other additions take the form of "penitential glosses" and can be found in the passages wherein the dying man talks about his misspent youth. Here Kurtz believes Hoccleve reveals something of his own timorous personality. The result is that the lofty Latin prose of Suso's *Horologium* has been decidedly humanized; that is, Hoccleve manages to give his work an individual touch.[30] At the end of the poem he appends a prose translation of the Ninth Lesson for All Hallows' Day.[31]

The *Ars Moriendi* literature is just one manifestation of the fifteenth century's obsession with the idea of death.[32] Lydgate's *Dance Macabre* consists of words spoken by Death to people whom he is leading to the grave, and of their responses. When Lydgate lay down his pen midway through the *Secrees of Old Philisoffres,* his last thoughts were of death: "Deth al consumyth / which may nat be denyed" (v. 1491). In the prologue to his Life of St. Anne, Osbern Bokenham[33] shows his awareness of the imminence of death. He fears that he has begun his work too late in life:

But sekyr I fere to gynne so late,
Lest men wolde ascryuen it to dotage.
For wel I know that fer in age
I am runne, & my lyues date
Aprochith fast, & the fers rage

[30] Yet Kurtz believes that "what is weak is almost invariably an addition or rendering of the poet's" (pp. 274-275). One has the feeling that Kurtz's evaluation of *Lerne to Dye* would be higher if Hoccleve had slavishly followed his original in a word-for-word prose translation. For further comments on Kurtz's opinions see Chapters III and IV.

[31] See Kurtz, "The Prose of Occleve's *Lerne to Dye,*" *MLN,* XXXIX (1924), 56-57.

[32] For a brief discussion of the attitude toward death in the fourteenth and fifteenth centuries, see Triggs's introduction to his edition of the *Assembly of Gods,* pp. xliii-l.

[33] *Legendys of Hooly Wummen,* ed. Mary S. Serjeantson, E.E.T.S., O.S., No. 206 (London, 1938 [for 1936]).

Of cruel deth — so wyl my fate
Ineuytable — hath at my gate
Set hys carte to carye me hens;
And I ne may ne can, thau I hym hate,
Ageyn hys fors make resistens.
[vv. 1407-16]

John Capgrave expresses thoughts of the same nature in the dedicatory epistle to his Commentary on the Creeds:

When the Psalmist saith: "According to Thy Name, so also is Thy praise," he speaks, I think, to me also, whose mind already is dull, and my body wrinkled, and, (as holy Job saith,) "my breath is weakened, my days are shortened, and only the tomb remains for me."

Affected by this consideration, I think every day whither I may direct my deeds, so that I may more easily return to that home from whence I was taken.[34]

And Hoccleve himself does not confine his meditations on death to the *Lerne to Dye* but writes in a vein similar to that of Bokenham and Capgrave in his *Dialogue with a Friend*:

"Of age am I fifty winter and thre;
Ripenesse of dethe / fast vpon me hastethe;
my lymes sumdell / now vnweldy be;
all my syght apperithe faste, and wastithe,
and my conceyte / a dayes now / not tastethe
as it hathe done / in yeres precedent;
now all a-nother is my sentement."
[vv. 246-252]

All things considered, one must agree with G. Gregory Smith that "*Timor mortis conturbat me* is the refrain of the century."[35] There is certainly nothing original in the subject matter of Hoccleve's *Lerne to Dye:* the poem is rather a representative expression of the *Zeitgeist*. It is significant in literary history because it is one of the earliest English versions of an *Ars Moriendi* and indeed the only Middle English rendition in verse. Moreover, in the humanization of the didactic portions and in the expansion of passages wherein the dying man laments his misspent youth, Hoccleve has managed to give an individual stamp to his *Lerne to Dye*.

6. NARRATIVE POETRY

Hoccleve first tried his hand at narrative poetry with some of the

[34] Included in the first appendix to Capgrave's *Book of the Illustrious Henries*, trans. Francis Charles Hingeston (London, 1858), p. 227.

[35] *The Transition Period* (Edinburgh and London, 1900), p. 14.

longer anecdotes, especially the Story of John of Canace, which he adapted from the *Liber de Ludo Scacchorum* in his *Regement of Princes.* But as a writer of narrative verse he is usually remembered for two poems based on stories in the *Gesta Romanorum,* namely, the *Tale of Jereslaus' Wife* and the *Tale of Jonathas.*

The *Gesta Romanorum* was probably the most popular collection of stories in medieval times. The definitive study of the work is by Hermann Oesterley, in the introduction to his monumental edition (Berlin, 1872). Important earlier studies are by Thomas Warton,[36] Francis Douce,[37] the Rev. Charles Swan,[38] and Sir Frederic Madden.[39] According to Oesterley, the *Gesta* was first compiled toward the end of the thirteenth century probably in England, whence it quickly spread to the continent (pp. 256 ff.). As early as the middle of the fourteenth century the various manuscripts had fallen into three groups: (1) an Anglo-Latin family, most completely represented by the fifteenth-century Brit. Mus. MS. Harl. 2270; (2) a family of Latin and German manuscripts that lie behind a German text printed at Augsburg in 1489; and (3) a family of continental manuscripts that form the basis of three Latin texts printed in the 1470's: (a) the *editio princeps,* consisting of 150 stories (or chapters), printed at Utrecht by Ketelaer and De Leempt; (b) a second edition, consisting of 151 chapters, printed at Cologne by Arnold Ter Hoernen; and (c) the so-called *Vulgärtext,* containing 181 chapters, printed at Cologne by Ulrich Zell. Oesterley's edition of the *Gesta* follows for the most part these three incunabula.

The question of which version of the *Gesta* Hoccleve used as the source for his two narrative poems has been a matter of much confusion. In discussing the *Tale of Jonathas,* Warton observes that Hoccleve "has literally followed the book before us, and has even translated into English prose the Moralisation annexed."[40] Earlier in the essay (p. v) he remarks that the book before him was a 1488 edition of the *Gesta* — an edition apparently resembling the *Vulgärtext* in the number and order of chapters and in all other essen-

[36] *A Dissertation on the Gesta Romanorum,* included in *The History of English Poetry . . . ,* III (London, 1781), i-xcvii.

[37] *A Dissertation on the Gesta Romanorum,* included in *Illustrations of Shakespeare . . . ,* II (London, 1807), 333-428.

[38] Introduction to his English translation of the *Gesta Romanorum,* rev. ed. (London, 1906).

[39] Introduction to his edition of *The Old English Versions of the Gesta Romanorum* (London, 1838).

[40] Warton's *Dissertation,* p. lvi.

tials. Warton's statement is misleading, if not downright inaccurate, because it can be shown that Hoccleve's immediate source was not a continental Latin version of the *Gesta* but rather a version belonging to the Anglo-Latin group. Douce pointed out the truth of the matter in 1807 — "Occleve's immediate model was our English *Gesta*"[41] — but his observation seems not to have been noticed by later Hoccleve scholars. Even Furnivall, in one of the forewords to his edition of Hoccleve's *Minor Poems,* is incorrect: "The Latin originals are in Oesterley's 1872 edition of the *Gesta*" (p. xlv). In most places where Hoccleve's narrative poems are mentioned, scholars refer loosely to the *Gesta Romanorum* as the poet's source without bothering to specify which *Gesta* they mean.

There are three mid-fifteenth-century English prose versions of the *Gesta* based on the Anglo-Latin manuscripts.[42] Wynkyn de Worde's early sixteenth-century volume of 43 *Gesta* stories is an English translation of Harl. MS. 5369, one of the manuscripts belonging to the Anglo-Latin family.[43] But with the exception of two stories from Harl. MS. 2270, which includes 102 stories, no Anglo-Latin text of the *Gesta* has ever been printed. The exceptions are as follows:

Harl. MS. 2270, No. 48, foll. 42r-44r. Celestinus in civitate Romana regnavit, prudens valde, qui habebat filiam pulchram. Included by Thomas Wright in *A Selection of Latin Stories,* Percy Society, Vol. VIII (London, 1842), pp. 114-121. (The story is a source of Shakespeare's *Merchant of Venice.*)

Harl. MS. 2270, No. 101, foll. 80r-82r. Menelaus in ciuitate Romana regnauit, qui filiam regis Hungarie in vxorem accepit. . . . Included by A. Wallensköld in *Le Conte de la Femme Chaste Convoitée par son Beau-frère,* Acta Societatis Scientiarum Fennicae, Vol. XXXIV, No. 1 (Helsingfors, 1907), pp. 111-116.

The former of these will not concern us here since it has nothing to do with Hoccleve. The latter, however, is the Anglo-Latin Story of Jereslaus' Wife. Hoccleve apparently used an Anglo-Latin text of the story practically identical with the text in Harl. MS. 2270. From the same manuscript I have transcribed the Story of Jonathas and Felicia ("Godfridus in civitate Romana regnavit prudens valde qui tres pueros habebat . . .") and included it in the first appendix to

[41] Douce's *Dissertation*, p. 390.

[42] Ed. by Madden (see n. 39 above) and later by Sidney J. H. Herrtage, E.E.T.S., E.S., No. 33 (London, 1879).

[43] See Oesterley, pp. 241-242.

my unpublished doctoral dissertation.[44] It can easily be shown that Hoccleve worked from an Anglo-Latin text identical with this one.

Even the most cursory comparison of Hoccleve's two narrative poems with the continental *Gesta* and the Anglo-Latin rendition shows clearly that Hoccleve worked from the latter. At the beginning of the continental Story of Jereslaus' Wife the emperor announces to his wife that he intends to visit the Holy Land and has arranged to leave the empire in her hands during his absence. He then sets out on his journey. In the Anglo-Latin version the empress replies to the words of her husband, who comforts her and then departs:

At illa: "Ex quo aliter non poterit esse, fiat voluntas vestra. Ego vero ero sicut turtur in vestra absentia, qui socium suum amisit, quia spero cum sanitate domum venietis." Imperator vero eam verbis dulcibus confortabat. Osculum ei tradidit et valefecit omnibus et ad Terram Sanctam perrexit [Wallensköld's transcription, p. 111].

Here is the parallel passage in Hoccleve's *Tale of Jereslaus' Wife:*

To whom / with spirit of humilitee,
She seide / "syn it is your good plesance
To departe hens / & / go to þat Contree,
I take moot algates, in souffrance,
Your wil / and shal, with hertes obeissance,
As treewe as turtle / þat lakkith hir feere
In your absence / I shal be / my lord deere.

"ffu1 sore I am agast, & greetly dreede
þat neuere yee shuln thennes with your lyf
Retorne / almighty god yow saue & speede!"
he to hir yaf wordes confortatyf
And kiste hir / and seide, "farewel, wyf!
Be nat abassht / ne nat dreedith, I preye;"
And foorth he hastith him in his iourneye.
[vv. 43-56]

Obviously Hoccleve follows the Anglo-Latin version, even to the extent of borrowing the simile involving the turtledove. One might note, however, that he expands the direct discourse somewhat and heightens its dramatic intensity. In this way he shows a certain amount of originality in the handling of his source.

Later on in the same story the empress and her brother-in-law become separated from a hunting party and are left alone in the forest

[44] "Thomas Hoccleve: His Traditionalism and His Individuality: A Study in Fifteenth-Century English Poetic" (Duke, 1965).

together. He tries to seduce her, but in vain. When he realizes that he cannot have his way, he disrobes her and leaves her hanging by her hair from a tree. The would-be seduction scene in the continental *Gesta* is just slightly more than half the length of the parallel material in the Anglo-Latin *Gesta,* and again it can be shown that Hoccleve obviously works from the latter (see vv. 197 ff.). In the Anglo-Latin version the empress and her brother-in-law both speak twice. Hoccleve translates the four speeches, augmenting the discourse to make the scene more dramatic. He also makes an effort to render the Latin into good idiomatic English: "Quid est hoc" becomes "What, fool." Again he reveals originality in the handling of his source.

The *Gesta* story on which the *Tale of Jereslaus' Wife* is based is a version of the Constance legend, which, in many different forms, was widely known throughout the Middle Ages.[45] It is best known today in the closely related versions of Chaucer (the Man of Law's Tale), Gower (*Confessio Amantis,* II, 587 ff.), and Trivet (Story of Constance, included in the Anglo-Norman *Chronicle*). Hoccleve's *Tale of Jereslaus' Wife* is apparently the first occurrence in English of the *Gesta* version of the legend.

A comparison of Hoccleve's *Tale of Jonathas* with the two Latin versions leads to a similar conclusion, namely, that Hoccleve's immediate source was the Anglo-Latin *Gesta.* With respect to the story itself, he makes no changes, no additions, and no omissions. But as in *Jereslaus' Wife,* he expands some of the direct discourse in the attempt to heighten the dramatic intensity of a scene. Additional bulk is the result of his occasional digressions from his source to offer personal commentary on the action. In these ways Hoccleve manages to give his work an individual flavor.[46]

7. RECURRENT THEMES

Many of Hoccleve's themes — such as the capriciousness of Fortune, youth and age, friendship, the world upside down, his lack of skill as a poet — are simply stock subjects on which a medieval writer was expected to show his versatility as a rhetorician. They are traditional motifs that occur throughout medieval literature and do not

[45] See Margaret Schlauch, *Chaucer's Constance and Accused Queens* (New York, 1927).

[46] For a thorough discussion of Hoccleve's handling of source material in his *Gesta Romanorum* poems, see Chapter IV.

necessarily reflect a writer's personal thoughts. On the other hand, Hoccleve's poetry often concerns itself with social and political problems of his times, undoubtedly reflecting his own thoughts and opinions. Much of this has already been pointed out and discussed by Wright, Furnivall, and others. Three extended passages, often alluded to, that relate to the contemporary scene occur in the Prologue to the *Regement of Princes* — the lines on the gaudy dress of the times (vv. 421 ff.), the mistreatment of the soldiers who had fought many years earlier in France (vv. 869 ff.), and the evils of ecclesiastical absenteeism (vv. 1401 ff.). The last passage is remarkable in that it is the only instance in all Hoccleve's works in which he openly criticizes the Church.

Two recurrent themes in Hoccleve demand careful consideration, the first being the question of heresy. In the Prologue to the *Regement of Princes* the Beggar describes to Hoccleve the burning of a heretic (vv. 281-322). Prince Henry was present at the "deedly castigacioun" and promised the man his life if he would return to the true faith. Before the fire was kindled the prince even ordered the sacrament to be brought to him in the hope that he would recant; but he doggedly stuck to his "oppynyoun dampnable" and was accordingly burned to death. The Beggar voices the hope that all heretics might be treated similarly. The burning of this particular heretic (a smith named John Badby) along with the prince's participation in the affair made an impression on other writers besides Hoccleve. Capgrave discusses the incident in his *Chronicle of England*.[47] A full account of the proceedings illustrated by an awe-inspiring engraving of the execution can be found in John Foxe's *Acts and Monuments*.[48]

Hoccleve returns again and again to the subject of heresy. In the *Balade to King Henry V on His Accession to the Throne* he urges the young king to be "holy chirches Champion" and to drive heresy out of the realm. In another *Balade to King Henry V* he refers to the king as a "werreyour ageyn the heresies bittir galle" and urges him to forbid public disputing about religious belief. Heresy is also the subject of the *Balade to the Knights of the Garter*. Hoccleve hopes that the knights will be able to "qwenche al this nusance" and drive the foes of Christ "to the outrance." In the *Balade After King Richard II's Bones Were Brought to Westminster* he deplores the

[47] Ed. Francis Charles Hingeston (London, 1858), p. 297.
[48] Ed. Stephen Reed Cattley, III (London, 1837), 235-239.

discord which heresy has brought to the realm. He earnestly hopes that King Henry V will be able to set things in order.

In the *Address to Sir John Oldcastle,* Hoccleve's lengthiest poem against heresy (see Section 3 above), Lucy Toulmin Smith sees "evidence of personal friendship."[49] She refers in particular to stanzas ii, iv, xiii, and lxii-lxiv. Apparently she bases her assertion simply on the apostrophes to Oldcastle found in these stanzas. But such evidence is flimsy. The apostrophe was a favorite rhetorical device of fifteenth-century poets, the use of which does not necessarily imply that any real connection existed between the poet and the person (or thing) apostrophized. Whether Hoccleve knew Sir John or not, he does show respect for him — as if he were well aware of the knight's other virtues. Other writers are not so kind as Hoccleve. Here, for example, is a stanza from the anonymous poem against the Lollards to which I referred in Section 3:

> Hit is vnkyndly for a kniȝt,
> þat shuld a kynges castel kepe,
> To bable þe bibel day & niȝt
> In restyng tyme when he shuld slepe;
> & carefoly awey to crepe,
> for alle þe chief of chiualrie.
> Wel aught hym to waile & wepe,
> þat suyche lust haþ in lollardie.
> [Robbins text, vv. 25-32]

The historian Capgrave gives a very unsympathetic account of Sir John in his *Chronicle of England.* At one place he emphasizes Oldcastle's bullheaded fanaticism: "A strong man in bataile he was, but a grete heretik, and a gret enmye to the Cherch. For his cause the archbishop gadered a Councel at London; for he sent oute prestis for to preche, whech were not admitted be non Ordinarie; and he was present at her sermones; and alle thei that seide ageyn his prestis was he redy to smite with his swerd" (p. 304). And in his account of Sir John's first trial Capgrave calls particular attention to the irreverent disrespect with which the knight viewed certain matters pertaining to the Church: "And whan thei asked him, what worchip he wold do to the ymage on the Crosse, he seide he wold wipe it, and kepe it clene. Than thei asked him what he seid of the Pope. He seid, 'The Pope is Antecrist; bischoppis be his membris and freres be his tayl' " (p. 306). Such was Sir John Oldcastle's

[49] In the introduction to her edition of the poem, *Anglia,* V (1882), 12.

reputation in the historical writings of the fifteenth century. With the change in religion in the next century, his tumultous life was restudied, the result being his elevation to blessed martyrdom.[50]

Sir John's reputation fell at the hands of Shakespeare — but this is a story too well known to need repeating here. In addition to the Falstaff plays one might mention *The First Part of the True and Honorable Historie of the Life of Sir John Oldcastle, the Good Lord Cobham,* an anonymous play, 1600; and John Weever's *Mirror of Martyrs, or The Life and Death of Sir John Oldcastle, Knight, Lord Cobham,* a long poem in six-line stanzas, 1601. The controversy regarding the knight continued into the seventeenth century. Richard James defended him from his Papal critics,[51] while Thomas Fuller tried to correct the grievous errors which had been perpetrated by "stage poets."[52] Even as late as 1880 Sir John was considered a subject suitable for poetry; see Tennyson's *Sir John Oldcastle, Lord Cobham.*

The *Address to Sir John Oldcastle* shows no remarkable degree of originality on Hoccleve's part, and it perhaps has little significance from a literary standpoint, but looked at historically it is certainly worthy of notice. It stands at the very beginning of a long religious controversy over the knight's character. It is the first of several literary works primarily concerned with his life and religious beliefs. It has a connection (albeit remote) with scholarship relating to the prototype of Shakespeare's Falstaff.

A second theme in Hoccleve which deserves attention is his attitude toward women. How can it be explained that he translated Christine de Pisan's *Epistre au Dieu d'Amours,* a passionate defense of women, and at the same time was capable of writing a highly satirical piece such as his *Humorous Praise of His Lady?* On this question it is helpful to compare Hoccleve's attitude toward women with that of Lydgate.

In reading through the latter's voluminous translations one discovers that Lydgate, whenever he discusses the fairer sex, speaks out

[50] See John Bale's *Brief Chronicle Concerning the Examination and Death of the Blessed Martyr of Christ, Sir John Oldcastle, the Lord Cobham* (London, [1548?]). Foxe praises him in *Acts and Monuments* (1564), and Holinshed (1577) calls him "a valiant captaine and a hardie gentle man."

[51] See James's notes to his transcription of Hoccleve's *Address to Sir John Oldcastle,* included in *The Poems, etc., of Richard James, B.D. (1592-1638),* ed. Alexander B. Grosart ([London], 1880), pp. 161-188.

[52] *The Church-History of Britain; From the Birth of Jesus Christ, Untill the Year M. DC. XLVIII* (London, 1655), p. 168.

of both sides of his mouth. Several examples of his ambiguous attitude can be pointed out in the *Troy Book*.[53] In Book I, verses 2072-96, he translates a passage of decidedly antifeminist sentiment in his source, Guido delle Colonne's *Historia Troiana*. He then apologizes for what he has written:

> þus liketh Guydo of wommen for tendite.
> Allas, whi wolde he so cursedly write
> Ageynes hem, or with hem debate!
> I am riȝt sory in englische to translate
> Reprefe of hem, or any euel to seye;
> Leuer me wer for her loue deye.
> [I. 2097-2102]

A similar apology occurs in the next book, immediately following another antifeminist passage which he pretends he had to translate:

> þus Guydo ay, of cursid fals delit,
> To speke hem harme haþ kauȝt an appetit,
> þoruȝ-oute his boke of wommen to seyn ille,
> þat to translate it is ageyn my wille.
> He haþ ay Ioye her honour to transuerse;
> I am sory þat I mote reherse
> þe felle wordis in his boke y-founde.
> [II. 3555-61]

One cannot help wondering why Lydgate took the trouble to English the antifeminist passages if he really was conscientiously opposed to such sentiments. A glance at the *Historia Troiana* suffices to show that he does not follow his source in all instances. If he omitted other material in the *Historia,* why then did he not omit the antifeminist passages? The obvious answer is that he did not want to. He has written his so-called apologies with tongue in cheek. Similar passages occur in *Reason and Sensuality*[54] and the *Fall of Princes*.[55] Alain Renoir is probably correct when he observes that one learns almost nothing about Lydgate's personal attitude toward women from either his conventional poems on courtly love or his avowedly antifeminist pieces, also highly conventional.[56] One is left, then,

[53] Ed. Henry Bergen, 4 vols., E.E.T.S., E.S., Nos. 97, 103, 106, 126 (London, 1906, 1908, 1910, 1935 [for 1920]).

[54] Ed. Ernst Sieper, 2 vols., E.E.T.S., E.S., Nos. 84, 89 (London, 1901, 1903). See vv. 6361-68.

[55] Ed. Henry Bergen, 4 vols. (Washington, 1923-27). See Bk. I, vv. 4719-46.

[56] "Lydgate's *Siege of Thebes*: A Study in the Art of Adaptation" (unpubl. diss. Harvard, 1955), pp. 100 ff.

with the passages in the above-mentioned translations. On the basis of them it appears to me that Lydgate's attitude toward women is primarily one of amusement. He delights in pointing out the foibles of the weaker sex, and he does so with good-humored irony. In his treatment of women he is very close to Chaucer.

Something of the good-humored approach can be seen in Hoccleve, especially in his *Humorous Praise of His Lady.* But as in the case of Lydgate's avowedly satirical poems, it would be unwise to read into the *Humorous Praise* much indication of Hoccleve's personal feelings toward women. The little piece should not be taken seriously. It is thoroughly conventional. It belongs to a distinct genre which Utley calls "the satirical panegyric of one's lady."[57] Utley points out several English poems in the same tradition, noting that prototypes can be found in Horace, Martial, and the Greek Anthology, the genre reaching its culmination in Shakespeare's Sonnet cxxx: "My mistress' eyes are nothing like the sun." He observes that Chaucer's *Complaint to His Purse* is a special development of the genre in that Chaucer pretends the purse is his "lady dere" and addresses it accordingly. He then classifies Hoccleve's *Humorous Praise* in the same sub-genre with Chaucer's *Complaint* under the assumption that the lady whom Hoccleve addresses is Lady Money. But this assumption does not have to be made. Hoccleve's *Humorous Praise of His Lady* is a roundel and immediately follows two other roundels, one of which *is* a complaint to Lady Money, while the other consists of her response. But nothing in the text of the *Humorous Praise* indicates that the lady should be equated with Lady Money. The poem belongs to the main genre rather than the sub-genre. Moreover, it is apparently the first *English* satirical panegyric of one's lady. Here are some typical lines:

> Hir bowgy cheekes been as softe as clay,
> with large Iowes and substancial.
> [vv. 6-7]
>
> Hir nose / a pentice is, þat it ne shal
> Reyne in hir mowth / thogh shee vp-rightes lay.
> [vv. 11-12]

Schirmer is undoubtedly right in suggesting that a parallel can be

[57] Francis Lee Utley, *The Crooked Rib: An Analytical Index to the Argument About Women in English and Scots Literature to the End of the Year 1568* (Columbus, Ohio, 1944), p. 45.

drawn between this poem and some of Skelton's verse.[58] *Elinor Rumming* is a good example of the same type of thing. It even outdoes Hoccleve's *Humorous Praise* in the grotesqueness of its descriptions.

Some of Hoccleve's clearly feminist writing is not devoid of an occasional bit of humor. One might cite, for example, this stanza from the *Letter of Cupid*:

> Al be it þat men fynde / o womman nyce,
> Inconstant / rechelees / or variable,
> Deynous / or prowd, fulfillid of malice,
> withoute feith or loue / & deceyuable,
> Sly / qweynte & fals / in al vnthrift coupable,
> wikkid and feers / & ful of crueltee,
> It folwith nat / swiche alle wommen be.
>
> [vv. 148-154]

The fallacy of making an unkind generalization about all women just because one or two are wicked was a popular feminist argument. But the way in which Hoccleve has presented the argument — that is, by listing a dozen disparaging adjectives describing the one wicked woman and then denying in a single line that they apply to all women — shows, perhaps, that he did not altogether lack a sense of humor.[59] It may be that passages like this offended the ladies of the court and caused Hoccleve's friend in the *Dialogue* to advise him to write, for a change, something in praise of women. But the *Letter of Cupid,* viewed as a whole, is at least as feminist in outlook as its French source. Following Christine, Hoccleve gives several examples of good women, including the Virgin Mary, and he frequently defends women with the popular argument *ad hominem,* which attributes the vicious antifeminist satires to the sensuality and frustration of wicked clerks. Later in the poem Hoccleve turns to the question of whether or not Eve was responsible for the fall of man. His answer is an emphatic No. His defense of Eve (vv. 351-378) is drawn partly from his source, but at verse 379 he begins a long digression in which he carries Christine's argument further. Eve "brak obedience," to be sure, but *men* continuously disobey God's commandments every day of their lives. In one respect Adam's was the greater sin:

[58] *Geschichte der Englischen und Amerikanischen Literatur von den Anfängen bis zur Gegenwart,* 2nd ed., I (Tübingen, 1954), 173.

[59] It should be noted, however, that in this stanza Hoccleve follows Christine's *Epistre* very closely (see Chapter III, p. 72).

They bothe weren in a cas semblable,
Sauf willyngly the feend deceyued Eeue;
So dide shee nat Adam / by your leeue.
[vv. 390-392]

At this point Hoccleve introduces the doctrine of the Fortunate Fall:

Yit was þat synne happy to man-kynde;
The feend deceyued was / for al his sleighte;
For aght he kowde him / in his sleightes wynde,
God, to descharge man-kynde of the weighte
Of his trespas / cam doun from heuenes heighte;
And flessh and blood he took of a virgyne,
And souffred deeth / man to deliure of pyne.
[vv. 393-399]

The passage is followed by three stanzas in praise of the Virgin that are reminiscent of Hoccleve's Marian hymns. The long digression ends with an apostrophe to St. Margaret immediately followed by the poet's comment that she is to be praised not so much for her virginity — "for ay We werreie ageyn chastitee" (v. 431) — but rather for her constancy. Twenty years later Hoccleve returned to the theme of constancy in the *Tale of Jereslaus' Wife,* a story clearly feminist in every respect.

Between the *Letter of Cupid* and the *Gesta* story, however, come two important discussions of women which occur as parts of longer works. In the last pages of the *Regement of Princes* Hoccleve relates several arguments designed to show that women are superior to men. First, the rib from which Eve was created was stronger and cleaner than Adam's clay. Moreover, the creation of woman, which took place inside Paradise, symbolizes the creation of Holy Church and its sacraments. Finally, Christ himself was born of a woman and served her "with right plesant corage" until his thirtieth year. Since woman is unquestionably the superior sex, man should always submit to her better judgment — even in the home:

If he & she shul dwellen in on house,
Goode is he suffre; therby pees may spring;
Housbondes pees is pesible suffryng.
[vv. 5192-94]

It was probably a statement like this which led Furnivall to exclaim, "Hoccleve was surely meant by nature to be under his wife's thumb."[60] In the *Dialogue with a Friend* Hoccleve returns to the

[60] Hoccleve's *Minor Poems,* p. xxxvii.

subject of woman's superiority. Having read only a portion of the *Letter of Cupid*, the Friend has mistakenly concluded that it is antifeminist in its total outlook. He urges Hoccleve to apologize for the supposed distress he has caused women and to write something in praise of them. He impresses upon him the futility of competing with the superior sex:

> "Adam begyled was with Eeues reed,
> And sikir so was shee by the Serpent,
> To whom god seide / 'this womman thyn heed
> Breke shal / for thurgh thyn enticement
> Shee hath y-broken my commandement.'
> Now, syn womman had of the feend swich might;
> To breke a mannes heed / it seemeth light."
> [vv. 722-728]

He tells him that if he wants "to lyue in ese" he should strive to please women and learn to take "in pacience" everything they say. In the last stanzas Hoccleve apologizes for a wrong he never committed and then launches into the *Tale of Jereslaus' Wife.*

Underneath the wit of the *Letter of Cupid* and the good-humored discussion of the *Regement* and the *Dialogue* one discovers a writer with a strongly feminist bias. The controversy over women was an extremely popular subject in the Middle Ages, and Hoccleve, unlike Chaucer and Lydgate, belongs clearly in the feminist camp. The *Tale of Jereslaus' Wife* is his supreme contribution to medieval feminist literature. One might even argue that his emphasis on the human attributes of the Virgin — something atypical of the new religious style of the fifteenth century — is partly owing to his feminist sympathies.

Josef Schick has observed that Lydgate's works "form a vast storehouse of mediaeval lore, many of the most popular sources of the knowledge of the Middle Ages being, in a greater or lesser degree, incorporated in them; and as they are mainly translations or compilations made evidently for the best-educated of his nation, they furnish ample illustration of what was then considered as the highest literary culture."[61] To a lesser extent Schick's remarks apply also to Hoccleve. Literary taste in England during the early part of the fifteenth century is clearly reflected in his courtly poetry, his manual of instruction for a prince, his political verse, his poems of

[61] Ed. Lydgate's *Temple of Glass*, E.E.T.S., E.S., No. 60 (London, 1891), p. xii.

solicitation, his religious lyrics, his *Ars Moriendi*, and his narrative poems. In his choice of subject matter Hoccleve fully realized what would be pleasing to an English public. He was no radical innovator in the *handling* of his subject matter, yet he sometimes managed to give his work an individual stamp. The bourgeois, realistic elements in the *Letter of Cupid* make it quite different from the courtly poetry of Lydgate. The *Regement of Princes* differs from other *regements* in its long Prologue full of autobiographical allusions and its concern with contemporary social and political problems. The religious lyrics emphasize the human attributes of the Virgin and are thus atypical of the new religious style of the fifteenth century. The *Regement*, the *Lerne to Dye*, and the two *Gesta* poems all contain many instances of Hoccleve's expansion and intensification of direct discourse taken from Latin sources. Thus, in small ways, Hoccleve does show his individuality, even when handling well-established traditional genres.

A study of Hoccleve's themes and genres reveals also that he is more important in literary history than has generally been assumed. His *Letter of Cupid* is the only English rendition of one of the best-known feminist works of the Middle Ages. His *Regement of Princes* is the first work in English to be drawn in part from the popular *Liber de Ludo Scacchorum*; it is one of the earliest appearances in English of extracts from the *Secreta Secretorum*; and it is the only widely known English rendition of material from Egidio Colonna's *De Regimine Principum*. His *Legend of the Virgin and Her Sleeveless Garment* is one of the very few English legends about Our Lady's Psalter. His *Lerne to Dye* is perhaps the first occurrence in English of any work of the *Ars Moriendi* variety; it is the only fifteenth-century poetical rendition. His two narrative poems, the *Tale of Jereslaus' Wife* and the *Tale of Jonathas*, are probably the first English versions of these particular *Gesta* stories. His *Humorous Praise of His Lady* is apparently the first English satirical panegyric of one's lady. From a historical perspective, then, Hoccleve is a writer who demands attention. Next to Lydgate and Caxton he was the most important disseminator of literary culture in fifteenth-century England.

CHAPTER III

STYLE

Any discussion of style in Middle English poetry must needs involve a discussion of the medieval rhetorical tradition, since to most medieval writers poetry was simply a branch of rhetoric. The classical distinction between poetry and rhetoric became blurred in post-classical times and in the Middle Ages, partly because the ancient poets, from Virgil on, "had practised with increasing zest all the rhetorical devices."[1] In fact, Geoffrey of Vinsauf's *Poetria Nova* (ca. 1210) is drawn in large part from the *Rhetorica ad Herennium*, a well-known post-classical treatise on rhetoric formerly attributed to Cicero.[2] In this connection it is important to observe that the *Ad Herennium,* in contrast with earlier, more catholic conceptions of rhetoric, places great emphasis on the more mechanical aspects of the subject, that is, the almost countless figures of speech and other verbal devices which medieval writers often refer to as the "colors of rhetoric." This conception of rhetoric, coupled with the ornate verbosity of the New Sophistic, became inextricably mixed with medieval theories of poetry, so that by the time of Geoffrey of Vinsauf — and indeed throughout the remainder of the Middle Ages — poetry was considered almost nothing more than versified rhetoric. Once in an age a genius, such as Chaucer, was able to master completely the

[1] J. W. H. Atkins, *English Literary Criticism: The Medieval Phase* (London, 1952), p. 29. For much of what follows in my paragraph I am indebted to Atkins and to J. M. Manly, "Chaucer and the Rhetoricians," *Proceedings of the British Academy*, XII (1926), 95-113. See also Edmond Faral, *Les Arts Poétiques du XIIe et du XIIIe Siècle: Recherches et Documents sur la Technique Littéraire du Moyen Age* (Paris, 1924); this contains Geoffrey of Vinsauf's *Poetria Nova.*

[2] I have consulted the Loeb Classical Library edition (Cambridge, Mass., and London, 1954). The parallel English translation is by Harry Caplan.

colors of rhetoric and use them for more worthy purposes. But most medieval poets, not gifted with the genius of a Chaucer, handled their conventional tools mechanically. In style, Thomas Hoccleve was very much a poet of his times.

Examples of the various traditional colors of rhetoric that Geoffrey of Vinsauf discusses in his *Poetria Nova* occur throughout Hoccleve's poetry. Of the eight basic methods of amplification (as expounded by Geoffrey) Hoccleve utilizes four extensively: apostrophe, personification, repetition, and digression.[3] Innumerable examples of apostrophe can be found in all the different genres Hoccleve mastered. In the religious lyrics he often calls on the Blessed Virgin, on Christ, or on the Apostle John; in the political poems and the poems of solicitation he addresses King Henry V, the Knights of the Garter, Sir John Oldcastle, and many other important personages; in the narrative poems he often inserts digressive material in the form of an apostrophe to one of the main characters; and in *La Male Regle* he addresses abstract concepts (such as Health and Flattery) and even includes an extended apostrophe to himself (vv. 351-392) in which he alludes to his want of money. This unusual last-named apostrophe is an example of Hoccleve's individual variation of a conventional rhetorical device.

Personification, like apostrophe, can be found on almost every page of his works. Of necessity it is involved in all apostrophes to inanimate objects or abstract concepts, but it occurs most frequently without apostrophe, as in these excerpts from the *Regement of Princes*:

> Than deemed I that seurete would nought
> With me abyde, it is nought to hir pay,
> Ther to soiurne as sche descende may
> [vv. 38-40]
>
> Pyte, I trowe, is beried, by my trouþe
> [v. 882]
>
> Oppressioun regneth in euery herne
> [v. 2541]

The first illustration is simply a run-of-the-mill personification about which there is nothing particularly remarkable. The next two, however, occur at climactic moments in the discussion. They are the final lines of their respective stanzas, and they give emphasis to and

[3] These four methods of amplification are present to a greater or lesser degree in the works of Lydgate, Bokenham, and other fifteenth-century poets.

elevate the foregoing material. Repetition in Hoccleve usually involves the expression of one simple idea by a pair of words ("trouthe and veritee," "trespas and offense," "beholde and see," etc.). But often it is a matter of the poet's finding two or more expressions for more extended ideas, as in the following "euphuistic" stanza from *La Male Regle*:

> Whil thy power / and excellent vigour
> (As was plesant vn-to thy worthynesse)
> Regned in me / & was my gouernour,
> Than was I wel / tho felte I no duresse,
> Tho farsid was I with hertes gladnesse;
> And now my body empty is, & bare
> Of ioie / and ful of seekly heuynesse,
> Al poore of ese / & ryche of euel fare!
> [vv. 9-16]

The word pair, however, is more frequent, probably because it is simpler. Indeed, it is one of the most noticeable features not only of Hoccleve's works but of Lydgate's as well (see below). As for digression, the examples are fewer in number than those of apostrophe, personification, and repetition; but digressive passages, often quite lengthy, comprise a large proportion of the total number of lines Hoccleve wrote. The *Letter of Cupid,* the *Gesta* tales, and the other poems in which he "translates" from a known source contain many digressive passages not to be found in the Latin or French (see Chapter IV). Other methods of amplification which Hoccleve utilizes to some extent include comparison (i.e., simile and analogy) and description of character.

In addition to the ways of expanding a subject, Geoffrey and other rhetoricians discuss various basic methods of abbreviation. These devices, however, were of less interest to most medieval writers, who, as Manly observed, were usually "not so much concerned to abbreviate as to amplify" (see n. 1 above). Lydgate makes use of *occupatio,* one of the principal means of abbreviation, in the *Siege of Thebes.*[4] Hoccleve often abbreviates by the exclusion of repetition and description — something immediately noticeable if one compares the relatively short *Letter of Cupid* with the original French of Christine de Pisan.

The medieval rhetoricians divided the numerous ornaments of

[4] Ed. Axel Erdmann, Pt. 1, E.E.T.S., E.S., No. 108 (London, 1911), vv. 1663 ff., 2426 ff., 4565 ff.

style into two groups, the "difficult" ornamental devices (*ornatus difficilis*) and the "easy" devices (*ornatus facilis*). The second group is subdivided into the figures of speech (*figurae verborum*) and the figures of thought (*figurae sententiarum*). Sometimes it is difficult to say just what the principles underlying the classification might have been; but in general it was thought that the difficult devices (or tropes) demanded more ingenuity on the part of the writer and were suited only to the high style, whereas the mechanical figures were more easily mastered and could be used advantageously in all three styles of writing — high, middle, and low. Hoccleve occasionally uses four of the difficult devices: hyperbole, metonymy, synecdoche, and onomatopoeia — the most striking example of onomatopoeia occurring in the *Tale of Jereslaus' Wife:*

> And shortly / of this for to speke and telle,
> The wynd ful sore / in the sail bleew & haf,
> And the wawes began to bolne & swelle,
> And our taklynge brast / and the ship claf
> In two / of seurtee loste y ny the staf.
> [vv. 911-915]

His favorite trope, however, is metaphor. All his poems are full of metaphorical expressions, many of them conventional and others less hackneyed, if not original. In comparing Hoccleve with Lydgate, one point in Hoccleve's favor is that his metaphorical conceits are never so extravagant that they are virtually unintelligible. This is sometimes the case in Lydgate's later religious poetry.[5] On the other hand modern critics would probably be dissatisfied with Hoccleve's use of metaphor and of imagery in general, because his approach is unsophisticated, mechanical, and typically medieval. That is, if one were to subject a Hoccleve poem to a minute imagistic study, one would be hard put to find any elaborate, premeditated organic design. Chaucer's works *will* respond to such an analysis, but they are exceptional. Hoccleve's art, like that of most medieval writers, is less subtle. His metaphorical conceits are decorative rather than functional.

Some of the figures of speech Hoccleve occasionally uses include *repetitio* (or anaphora), *gradatio* (or epanastrophe), *contentio* (or antithesis of words), and *interpretatio* (or the repetition of an idea

[5] See Walter F. Schirmer, *John Lydgate: A Study in the Culture of the XVth Century,* trans. Ann E. Keep (Berkeley and Los Angeles, 1961), pp. 75-76.

in different words). But his favorite "easy" ornamental device is the rhetorical question, which he often uses in conjunction with apostrophe:

O Oldcastel / allas / what eilid thee
To slippe in to the snare of heresie?
[*Address to Sir John Oldcastle,* vv. 25-26]

Sometimes the rhetorical questions are of a type which Geoffrey calls *ratiocinatio* (i.e., a question addressed by a speaker to himself):

Allas, what hath pryde profytid me,
Or what am y bet / for riche richesse hepynge?
[*Lerne to Dye,* vv. 197-198]

Why sette y so myn herte in Vanitee?
O, why ne had y lerned for to die?
Why was y nat ferd of goddes maugree?
What eilid me / to bathe in swich folie?
[*Ibid.,* vv. 281-284]

Hoccleve has a fondness also for proverbial material. For purposes of convenience I shall adopt the usual threefold division of proverbial material — full-fledged proverbs, proverbial phrases, and sententious remarks — although I recognize that the lines of demarcation are sometimes rather faint.[6] As might be expected, Hoccleve's didactic *Regement of Princes* and the didactic passages in the autobiographical poems are full of sententious remarks. Hoccleve also occasionally intersperses his narrative poems with *sententiae.* Here are three examples from the *Tale of Jereslaus' Wife:*

And sikirly / where as þat no credence
May been had / wysdam conseillith silence.
[vv. 426-427]

Lo, thogh god him / to wreke a whyle abyde,
The fals and wikkid, qwytith he sum tyde.
[vv. 699-700]

Be nat abassht / it manly is to synne,
But feendly is / longe lye ther-ynne.
[vv. 783-784]

Placed as they are at the end of their respective rhyme-royal stanzas, these *sententiae* are in the form of couplets. All three constitute additions Hoccleve has made to his source. The Latin words written in the margin of Durham MS. Cosin V. III. 9 beside the

[6] See B. J. Whiting, "The Nature of the Proverb," *Harvard Studies and Notes in Philology and Literature,* XIV (1932), 273-307.

third example — "humanum est peccare" — do not appear in the Anglo-Latin version of the story.

Geoffrey of Vinsauf includes *sententia* among the thirty-four figures of speech. He does not list the proverb either as a figure of speech or a figure of thought, although he observes that it is often used when a writer begins a story artificially by plunging *in medias res.* Since Hoccleve, following his source, begins the two *Gesta* tales *ab ovo,* there would be no precedent for his using an introductory proverbial statement. Occasionally, however, in other places of a poem, he does use a full-fledged proverb as distinct from a *sententia,* as in this example from the *Letter of Cupid:*

> An old prouerbe seid is in englissh:
> Men seyn þat brid or foul is deshonest,
> what so it be / and holden ful cherlissh,
> Þat wont is to deffoule his owne nest.
> [vv. 183-186]

Proverbial phrases can also be pointed out, some of them of the comparison variety and others like the two following examples from the *Complaint:*

> farwell my sorow / I caste it to the cok
> [v. 386]

> and he me gave a bone / on for to knawe
> [v. 398]

Hoccleve does not use proverbs, proverbial phrases, and *sententiae* in an especially subtle or individual fashion. Unlike Chaucer and some of the anonymous dramatists, he never uses proverbial material as a means of characterization.[7] To him a proverb or a *sententia* is simply a decorative device, or an easy and effective way of imparting moral exhortation, or a means of filling out a rhyme-royal stanza.

Of Geoffrey's nineteen figures of thought Hoccleve utilizes about half, some of which I have alluded to in the foregoing discussion. The list includes *conformatio* (personification), *diminutio* (self-disparagement), *exemplum* (illustrative story), *expolitio* (enlarging on a topic in different ways), *frequentatio* (accumulation of arguments or facts), *imago* (comparison), *licentia* (bold or censorious speech — something Hoccleve uses very infrequently), *notatio* (de-

[7] Chaucer uses proverbs in his characterization of Pandarus; see B. J. Whiting, *Chaucer's Use of Proverbs,* Harvard Studies in Comparative Literature, XI (Cambridge, Mass., 1934), pp. 3-4. See also Whiting's *Proverbs in the Earlier English Drama,* Harvard Studies in Comparative Literature, XIV (Cambridge, Mass., 1938), p. x.

scription of character), and *similitudo* (simile). Most of Hoccleve's *exempla* occur in the *Regement of Princes*; and, as I noted in the last chapter, they account for approximately 1,000 lines of the poem. None of the other figures of thought deserves special comment except *diminutio*.

On several occasions Hoccleve calls attention to his supposed lack of ability as a poet:

> Mi dere maistir — god his soule quyte! —
> And fadir, Chaucer, fayn wolde han me taght;
> But I was dul, and lerned lite or naght.
> [*Regement of Princes*, vv. 2077-79]

> I dreede lest þat my maister Massy
> Þat is of fructuous intelligence,
> Whan he beholdith how vnconnyngly
> My book is metrid / how raw my sentence
> How feeble eek been my colours, his prudence
> Shal sore encombrid been of my folie.
> [*Balade to the Duke of Bedford*, vv. 10-15]

> If þat I in my wrytynge foleye,
> As I do ofte, (I can it nat withseye,)
> Meetrynge amis / or speke vnfittyngly,
> Or nat by iust peys / my sentences weye,
> And nat to the ordre of endytyng obeye,
> And my colours sette ofte sythe awry,
> With al myn herte wole I buxumly
> It to amende and to correcte, him preye;
> For vndir his correccioun stande y.
> [*Balade to My Gracious Lord of York*, vv. 46-54]

Hoccleve's disparagers have taken great delight in pointing out passages such as these. One should be aware, however, that similar passages can be pointed out in the works of Ashby, Bokenham, Scogan, Walton, Lydgate, and even Chaucer. The question that arises is whether the frequent verses of self-deprecation in Middle English poetry are sincere expressions of regret or, rather, pure convention. Probably none of the passages should be taken at face value. Curtius examined self-deprecation from the time of Cicero to the end of the Middle Ages, concluding that the almost countless protestations of inadequacy are affected, that they are conventional rhetorical formulas, and that they constitute one of the many *topoi* at the disposal of ancient and medieval writers.[8] Hoccleve's verses

[8] Ernst Robert Curtius, *European Literature and the Latin Middle Ages*, trans. Willard R. Trask (New York, 1953), pp. 83-85.

of self-deprecation, then, should not be examined in isolation but approached in the context of a tradition that extends from classical times to his own day. One certainly cannot dismiss him as a poet of no importance simply because he *pretends* to certain shortcomings, metrical and otherwise.

Geoffrey of Vinsauf does not discuss meter, stanzaic patterns, rhyme, handling of sources, aureate diction, and syntax. He has very little to say about alliteration, stopgap expressions, and word pairs. Since the last three items are related to the material just discussed, that is, the so-called easy ornamental devices, I shall take them up at this point. Alliteration is discussed briefly in the *Rhetorica ad Herennium.* Chaucer occasionally uses it as either an ornamental device or a means of heightening a normally stressed syllable or word which happens to fall in a metrically unstressed position.[9] But his use of the figure is decidedly infrequent in comparison with that of Lydgate and Hoccleve. Examples of various alliterative patterns in Hoccleve's verse have been meticulously collected by Alfons Häcker and classified according to the number of alliterative letters, their positions in the line, and so forth.[10] Both Hoccleve and Lydgate use alliteration primarily as an ornamental device and as a means of achieving emphasis. Perhaps its frequent appearance in fifteenth-century verse owes something to the alliterative revival of the preceding century and thus represents a harking back to native traditions.

Another aspect of late medieval style that deserves comment is the use of stopgap expressions. They are very frequent in Lydgate's poetry. Sieper and Locock have called attention to them and divided them into well-defined groups, such as assertions of truth, allusions to a source, and adverbial expressions of time.[11] Miss Locock decries verse (in this case Lydgate's) that abounds with such "inanities." Even the editors of the *Life of Our Lady,* who usually speak quite favorably of Lydgate, admit that his "use of 'stop-gap' expressions seems to have no other justification than the desire to

[9] See Paull F. Baum, *Chaucer's Verse* (Durham, N.C., 1961), pp. 55-60.

[10] *Stiluntersuchung zu T. Hoccleves poetischen Werken* (diss. Marburg, 1914), pp. 19-26.

[11] Lydgate's *Reson and Sensuallyte,* ed. Ernst Sieper, Pt. 1, E.E.T.S., E.S., No. 84 (London, 1901), pp. 54-56; and his *Pilgrimage of the Life of Man,* ed. F. J. Furnivall and Katharine B. Locock, Pt. 3, E.E.T.S., E.S., No. 92 (London, 1904), pp. xliv-xlvii.

fill out the measure of his verse."[12] Whether these conventional expressions can be justified from an artistic standpoint or not, they do exist and are a very noticeable stylistic feature of much early fifteenth-century poetry. They can be found not only in Lydgate but also in Hoccleve (to a lesser extent) and other poets of the age. They are especially noticeable in the popular tail-rhyme romances.

In the two *Gesta* poems Hoccleve has borrowed some of the conventional expressions that one immediately associates with tail-rhyme romances.[13] Sometimes he summons his audience to attention in the fashion of a medieval minstrel: "But herkneth how shee baar hire aftirward" (*Jonathas*, v. 406) and "Now herkneth / how it hire made smerte" (*ibid.*, v. 663). Like the popular minstrel he occasionally directs attention to his source: "Nathelees / of this tretith nat the book" (*Jereslaus' Wife*, v. 264), "The booke maketh no mencion of that" (*ibid.*, v. 430), and "thus seith the booke sanz faill" (*Jonathas*, v. 665). Sometimes he fills out a line with an assertion of the truth: "withouten lye" (*Jereslaus' Wife*, v. 94), "withoute dreede" (*ibid.*, v. 124), "withouten ooth" (*Jonathas*, v. 99), "and ther shal be no nay" (*ibid.*, v. 208), and " 'Modir, right this,' seide he / 'nat wole y lye: / ffor soothe, modir / my ryng is ago' " (*ibid.*, vv. 259-260). Again like the minstrel he often makes use of various adverbial expressions of time: "Withoute any delay or taryynge" (*Jereslaus' Wife*, v. 504), "And withoute delay / to hire he sterte" (*ibid.*, v. 932), "But I no whyle may with yow abyde" (*Jonathas*, v. 540), and "No lengere there thought to abyde" (*ibid.*, v. 668). All of these hackneyed expressions are formulaic and usually associated with popular poetry. They were a convenient means by which a medieval minstrel, reciting his verse in a noisy innyard to an unsophisticated audience, could hold his audience's attention, provide a slowing of pace, and fill out bothersome lines and stanzas.

One of the most curious features of fifteenth-century verse is that poets often resorted to hackneyed, conventional stopgap expressions while, at the same time, they consciously strove for a grandiose style

[12] Lydgate's *Life of Our Lady*, ed. Joseph A. Lauritis, Ralph A. Klinefelter, and Vernon F. Gallagher (Pittsburgh, 1961), p. 213.

[13] The best studies of the tail-rhyme romances are Eugen Kölbing's introduction to his edition of *Amis and Amiloun* (Heilbronn, 1884) and A. McI. Trounce, "The English Tail-rhyme Romances," *Medium Aevum*, I (1932), 87-108, 168-182; II (1933), 34-57, 189-198; III (1934), 30-50.

through elaborate rhetorical devices and aureate diction. The word pair, essentially a method of amplification, is an unusual poetical device because it works both ways. Like the medieval minstrel Hoccleve often uses word pairs simply to eke out lines with a minimum of effort. Many of them are formulaic and belong definitely to the realm of stopgap expressions. On the other hand, they often conduce to dignity, copiousness, and sonority of expression and thus serve the function of heightening the style.[14] In many cases Hoccleve utilizes word pairs obviously with the idea of producing an ostentatious literary effect.

Unfortunately for Hoccleve's reputation, the use of word pairs has gone out of fashion since his day, and, as a result, his workmanship has been decried by many scholars. Kurtz refers contemptuously to the abundance of word pairs — Hoccleve's "besetting sin" — in *Lerne to Dye.* He remarks that "other poets of the age use the device more rarely" and believes that Hoccleve "contracted the habit in his scrivening of legal documents."[15] Kurtz's critique is most unfair to Hoccleve because it does not attempt to view his poetry in the context of other medieval literature. Hoccleve was neither the first nor the last English writer to commit the "sin" of using word pairs. *Some* poets of the age may have used them "more rarely," but certainly not Lydgate, who used them even more frequently than did Hoccleve. A study of the place of word pairs in medieval literature may not lead to a justification of the so-called sin on artistic grounds. It may not persuade anyone to like Hoccleve's poetry. But it does lead to a better understanding and a more mature appreciation of this aspect of his style.

Word pairs were not invented by either Hoccleve, Chaucer, or earlier Middle English writers who, according to some scholars, often tried to make a French word intelligible by pairing it off with a native English word.[16] Many examples of word pairs occur in the Anglo-Saxon translation of Bede's *Ecclesiastical History,* and they are often used to express a single word in the original Latin.[17] A few

[14] See James Bradstreet Greenough and George Lyman Kittredge, *Words and Their Ways in English Speech* (New York, 1905), p. 115.

[15] Benjamin P. Kurtz, "The Relation of Occleve's *Lerne to Dye* to Its Source," *PMLA*, XL (1925), 267-268.

[16] See Oliver Farrer Emerson, "Prof. Earle's Doctrine of Bilingualism," *MLN*, VIII (1893), 202-206.

[17] See J. M. Hart, "Rhetoric in the Translation of Bede," included in *An English Miscellany: Presented to Dr. Furnivall in Honour of His*

English writers after the Conquest may have consistently coupled French with English words, but not Chaucer. In the Prologue to the *Canterbury Tales*, and indeed in all Chaucer's works, there are three types of word pairs: (1) one French and one English, (2) both English, and (3) both French.[18] The same can be said about many English works after Chaucer. Clearly, then, Hoccleve's coupling of synonymous words from two languages is not necessarily a result (as Kurtz would have us believe) of his copying legal documents in the Privy Seal. Although both Hoccleve and Lydgate used word pairs much more extensively than did Chaucer and other earlier writers, there were other early fifteenth-century writers who favored the device, and the use of it by no means came to an end with the death of Lydgate. Bokenham uses word pairs occasionally in the *Legendys of Hooly Wummen*[19] and quite often in the prose of his *Mappula Angliae*.[20] They also crop up frequently in some of Caxton's prefaces (late fifteenth century) and in some of the best-known prayers of the *Book of Common Prayer* (1549 and 1552).

Hoccleve has been criticized by Kurtz and other scholars for using word pairs primarily as an easy means of filling out difficult lines. In many cases this is undoubtedly true. Yet mere ease in versification is not the *raison d'être* of word pairs in English literature. I have already noted that they occur in the Anglo-Saxon *Ecclesiastical History*, which, of course, is in *prose*. One might also recall that Chaucer uses word pairs in his prose translation of Boethius' *Consolation of Philosophy*, two English words often expressing a single word in the original Latin. [21] The device is also found in the prose of Cranmer, Caxton, Bokenham, and even Hoccleve himself. The prose ending of the *Lerne to Dye*, for example, is full of word pairs which often translate a single word in Heinrich Suso's Latin.[22] Old

Seventy-fifth Birthday (Oxford, 1901), pp. 150-154. For another useful study of word pairs see L[eon] Kellner, "Abwechselung und Tautologie: Zwei Eigenthümlichkeiten des Alt- und Mittelenglischen Stiles," *Englische Studien*, XX (1895), 1-24.

[18] Emerson, pp. 203-204; see also Fritz Karpf, *Studien zur Syntax in den Werken Geoffrey Chaucers*, Pt. 1, Wiener Beiträge zur Englischen Philologie, LV (Vienna, 1930), pp. 103 ff.

[19] Ed. Mary S. Serjeantson, E.E.T.S., O.S., No. 206 (London, 1938 [for 1936]).

[20] Ed. C[arl] Horstmann, *Englische Studien*, X (1887), 1-34; see especially chap. xvii.

[21] See Karpf, p. 104.

[22] Benjamin P. Kurtz, "The Prose of Occleve's *Lerne to Dye*," *MLN*, XXXIX (1924), 56-57.

and Middle English prose translators evidently felt that a single English word would not suffice to convey the full meaning of the corresponding Latin word. Likewise writers who composed original prose works evidently felt that one word would not be sufficient to express a complete idea. Therefore they resorted to word pairs. The desire for complete and exact expression is probably just as important a factor in the occurrence of word pairs in poetry as the desire for an easy means of eking out a line. Also, many word pairs contain one or even two sonorous Latinate terms which give additional dignity to a work, whether in prose or verse.

Word pairs are usually classified in two different ways. Sometimes, as already indicated, they are divided into three groups according to the etymology of the two words involved. Sometimes they are classified according to the meanings of the words. Many word pairs, for example, consist of two synonymous terms. Others consist of two words having similar, different, or even opposite meanings. Occasionally one term represents a general idea, in which the other is included in the relation of species to genus. Countless examples of the various types in both systems of classification can be pointed out in the poetry of Hoccleve. For the present discussion, however, I shall classify word pairs *according to their position in the line.* This method has the advantage of showing that Hoccleve, even though he uses word pairs to an unusually great extent, at least tries to achieve some degree of syntactical variety. Examples of the device may be divided into the following groups:

Type A_1. Two terms connected usually by "and" or "or" appear at the end of a verse. This is the most common type.

Of men þat doon hem outrage & offense
[*Letter of Cupid,* v. 12]

And with so pitous cheere and contenance
[*Ibid.,* v. 23]

whyles my lyf may lasten & endure
[*Ibid.,* v. 31]

A man him-self to accuse & diffame
[*Ibid.,* v. 65]

Type A_2. Two terms connected by "and" or "or" appear in positions other than the end of the verse.

Bytakynge and committynge vn-to thee
[*Jereslaus' Wife,* v. 29]

And thanne she spak / and seide in this wyse
[*Ibid.*, v. 772]

But a lady of excellent beautee
Allone and soul / cam by the way rydynge
[*Ibid.*, vv. 887-888]

Me to socoure and helpe . . .
[*Ibid.*, v. 894]

Type B. Both terms have modifiers or other accompanying words.

It is eek of swich vertu and swich kynde
[*Jonathas*, v. 107]

ffor to þat ende and to þat entente
[*Ibid.*, v. 165]

In honur and in mynde of the gladnesse
[*Miracle of the Virgin*, v. 51]

How good clothyng and how fressh apparaille
[*Ibid.*, v. 72]

Type C. One or more words come between the first term and the coordinate conjunction. This might be called an unbalanced word pair.

At instance of thy blessid sone and deere
[*Ad Patrem*, v. 48]

For whan his body scourgid was & bete
[*Ibid.*, v. 71]

For aght they kowde rebuke him or threte
[*Ibid.*, v. 73]

Þat hath in loue / spent his tyme & vsid
[*Letter of Cupid*, v. 121]

Type D. The first term appears at the end of one line and the second at the beginning of the next line. This might be called a staggered word pair. It is very infrequent.

. . . and of pitee
And routhe meeued / hire adoun took he
[*Jereslaus' Wife*, vv. 860-861]

. . . for þat men sholde caste
And suppose / how þat no wight but shee
[*Ibid.*, vv. 880-881]

. . . þat no thyng þat man may thynke
Or speke . . .
[*Ad Patrem*, vv. 16-17]

. . . o verray sustenour
And piler of our feith . . .
[*Balade to King Henry V*, vv. 12-13]

Various combinations of one or more of the four types often appear in successive lines.

> But thy sone / on the crois þat starf and dyde
> For our trespas and oure iniquitee
> [*Ad Patrem,* vv. 65-66]
>
> Our soules lurkyng / sores and langour,
> with thy brennyng dart and thy loues broond,
> Visite and helpe . . .
> [*Ad Spiritum Sanctum,* vv. 19-21]
>
> Thow graunte vs grace thee to plese & qweeme,
> And to thy wil and plesaunce vs gouerne,
> Our seekly freeltee beholde and concerne
> [*Ibid.,* vv. 31-33]
>
> Clensere of our gilt and iniquitee,
> Releeuere of hem þat doun slippe and slyde,
> Ground of meeknesse, & destroyour of pryde
> [*Ibid.,* vv. 47-49]

Word pairs such as the examples above are not fortuitous tautologies which Hoccleve dashed off at times when he was too lazy to do anything better. They are certainly not the result of the normal prolixity that accompanies old age, as one writer suggested in the case of Lydgate.[23] Rather, they are a conventional means of literary embellishment which Hoccleve, Lydgate, and others consciously employed and systematically worked out in a variety of ways. There is no doubt that medieval writers looked on word pairs as a highly desirable mode of expression both in verse and in prose.

Two aspects of medieval poetic, diction and syntax, deserve attention because they are areas in which Hoccleve's practice differs from that of Lydgate. Lydgate's name is always associated with a type of diction most often described with the adjective "aureate."[24] His works are full of sonorous, polysyllabic words of Romance derivation which he consciously used to elevate his style to the highest possible level. Approximately 850 Romance words appear, so far as we know, for the first time in Lydgate's poetry.[25] Two-thirds of

[23] Sieper, p. 50.

[24] See Elfriede Tilgner, *Die Aureate Terms als Stilelement bei Lydgate,* Germanische Studien, CLXXXII (Berlin, 1936).

[25] Georg Reismüller, *Romanische Lehnwörter (Erstbelege) bei Lydgate: Ein Beitrag zur Lexicographie des Englischen im XV. Jahrhundert,* Münchener Beiträge zur Romanischen und Englischen Philologie, XLVIII (Leipzig, 1911); see also Joseph Mersand, *Chaucer's Romance Vocabulary* (Brooklyn, 1937), p. 49.

these are still in current usage, while the others seem never to have been really a part of the language. All are frequently referred to as Lydgate's "aureate terms."

In one of the first comprehensive studies of late medieval diction, John Cooper Mendenhall defines aureate terms as "those new words, chiefly Romance or Latinical in origin, continually sought, under authority of criticism and the best writers, for a rich and expressive style in English, from about 1350 to about 1530."[26] This definition, however, is too broad, because it implies that virtually every French or Latinate word introduced by Chaucer, Gower, Hoccleve, and Lydgate was an aureate term. Many Romance words do appear in writing for the first time in Chaucer's poetry. They are fresh, novel, and literary, and they undoubtedly seemed so to Chaucer's audiences; but they are not necessarily aureate. Lydgate's remarkable diction (which *is* aureate) is a result of the exaggeration beyond all reasonable limits of what are only tendencies in Chaucer's verse (especially *An ABC*). Lydgate's sonorous polysyllabic words, often appearing in clusters, serve an almost exclusively decorative function. They are a "verbal gilding of literary style," to borrow an expression from Mendenhall. Schirmer remarks that "as a result of the example set by Lydgate, this 'poetic diction' came to predominate in fifteenth-century verse" (p. 74).

We must now turn to Hoccleve's place in the development of post-Chaucerian poetic diction. According to the *Oxford English Dictionary,* several words of Romance derivation occur apparently for the first time in his works, three examples being *beneuolence* (*Mother of God,* v. 10), *inconstant* (*Letter of Cupid,* vv. 101, 149), and *impressioun* (*ibid.,* v. 233 — in the now obsolete sense of "an attack or assault"). If one looked up all Hoccleve's Romance words in the *Oxford English Dictionary,* one could no doubt find more *Erstbelege* — but probably not many more. Words such as *affeccion, amiable, assaille, asswage, bareyne, benigne, coupable, debonaire, deceyuable, deuout, deynous, discreet, dissimulen, excusacion, greuance, habitacioun, humilitee, malice, mesurable, pitous, possessioun, sclaundre,* and *unweeldy* — all to be found in the *Letter of Cupid* — had already been introduced in the thirteenth and fourteenth centuries. Since most of these words had been in the language for a generation or more, they probably did not seem

[26] *Aureate Terms: A Study in the Literary Diction of the Fifteenth Century* (Lancaster, Pa., 1919), p. 12.

fresh or unusual to Hoccleve's public; they could hardly be called aureate.

The percentage of French words in the *Letter of Cupid* is higher than in Hoccleve's other works. The mere fact that an English work is a translation or paraphrase from the French does not necessarily mean that Romance diction is prominent. Chaucer's *Book of the Duchess,* based on French sources, contains a relatively low percentage of Romance words.[27] This is not the case, however, with the *Letter of Cupid.* Sometimes Hoccleve follows Christine so closely that his verse might well be described as aureate:

Al be it þat men fynde / o womman nyce,
Inconstant / rechelees / or variable,
Deynous / or prowd, fulfillid of malice,
withoute feith or loue / & deceyuable,
Sly / qweynte & fals / in al vnthrift coupable,
wikkid and feers / & ful of crueltee,
It folwith nat / swiche alle wommen be.

[vv. 148-154]

. . . but they been charitable,
Pitous / deuout / ful of humilitee,
Shamefast / debonaire and amiable . . .

[vv. 345-347]

Et supposé qu'il en y ait de nyces
Ou remplies de pluseurs divers vices,
Sanz foy n'amour ne nulle loiaulté,
Fieres, males, plaines de cruaulté,
Ou pou constans, legieres, variables,
Cautelleuses, fausses et decevables,
Doit on pour tant toutes mettre en fremaille
Et tesmoignier qu'il n'est nulle qui vaille?

[vv. 185-192]

Car nature de femme est debonnaire,
Moult piteuse, paourouse et doubtable
Humble, doulce, coye et moult charitable,
Amiable, devote . . .

[vv. 672-675]

But these passages are exceptional. Hoccleve does use words of Romance derivation to some extent in all his poems, but they seldom come in clusters. They are not strange, overly dulcet, or laboriously artificial. Even the *Letter of Cupid,* with its high percentage of Romance words, does not approach in aureate diction a poem such as Lydgate's *Ballade at the Reverence of Our Lady, Qwene of Mercy.*[28] In diction Hoccleve is much closer to Chaucer than Lydgate. The author of the fifteenth-century *Book of Courtesy* described Hoc-

[27] See Mersand, pp. 75-78.

[28] The poem is analyzed by Schirmer in "Der Stil in Lydgates Dichtung," included in his *Kleine Schriften* (Tübingen, 1950), pp. 40-56.

cleve's language with the adjective "playne."[29] It is obviously plain beside the "termes curious and sentacious" of Lydgate.

Hoccleve's syntax has never received thorough study.[30] The most noticeable characteristic to a modern reader is the endless number of lines containing inverted word order, as in these typical examples selected at random from the *Tale of Jereslaus' Wife:* "And vndir thee / my brothir heer shal be" (v. 31), "Haaste I me wole / fro thennes away" (v. 42), "That thow me kneew / thow blisse shalt the tyde" (v. 532), and "That he vn-to yow / nat entende may" (v. 602). Of course Hoccleve has not done anything unprecedented. Inverted word order is traditional in Middle English verse; it can be found in Chaucer, Lydgate, and all the tail-rhyme romances. The influence of French word order is one explanation for it, poetic license another, and the demands of meter and rhyme a third. Some examples of inverted word order in Middle English are possibly vestiges of the earlier state of the language.[31]

In one respect Hoccleve's syntax differs from Lydgate's. Almost everyone who has written about Lydgate has called attention to his loose syntax. "Drawled-out and incompact," Schick remarks, "are the first epithets which one would most readily apply to the style of the monk's productions. His sentences run on aimlessly, without definite stop, and it is often difficult to say where a particular idea begins or ends. One certainly has the impression that the monk never knew himself, when he began a sentence, how the end of it would turn."[32] A good way to appreciate the difficulty of Lydgate's syntax is to read the recent edition of the *Life of Our Lady* (see n. 12 above), which has been given no editorial punctuation. But even the most carefully punctuated texts of his works are often ambiguous in syntax. One cannot say for certain whether the ambiguity is a result of his ignorance in grammar, or his misfortune in having his works copied by careless scribes, or his belief that loose syntax and rambling sentences, along with aureate diction, would help produce an elevated style. Whatever the case may be, the point of this dis-

[29] Ed. Frederick J. Furnivall, E.E.T.S., E.S., No. 3 (London, 1868), v. 360.

[30] For a limited study see Eduard Buchtenkirch, *Der syntaktische Gebrauch des Infinitiv in Occleve's De Regimine Principum* (diss. Jena, 1889).

[31] On this question see André Courmont, *Studies on Lydgate's Syntax in the Temple of Glas*, Bibliothèque de la Faculté des Lettres, XVIII (Paris, 1912), pp. 120-125.

[32] Lydgate's *Temple of Glass*, ed. Josef Schick, E.E.T.S., E.S., No. 60 (London, 1891), p. cxxxiv.

cussion is simply that loose syntax is a fault of which Thomas Hoccleve cannot be accused. In all his verse there is hardly a single instance of syntactical ambiguity.

In summary, Hoccleve's style is best understood and appreciated in the context of other fifteenth-century literature. The rhetorical nature of his poetry is understandable in view of the fact that the Middle Ages defined poetry as versified rhetoric. His use of word pairs is a conspicuous feature of his style because the word pair was considered a highly desirable ornamental device throughout the fifteenth century. Unlike Lydgate, he does not revel in aureate diction. Again unlike Lydgate, he has no loose, incoherent syntax. The originality he occasionally reveals can best be seen when one compares his works with their sources; but this is the subject of the next chapter.

CHAPTER IV

HANDLING OF SOURCES

An examination of Hoccleve's works in comparison with their originals throws additional light on his poetic technique. Kurtz has already made such a study with regard to the *Lerne to Dye*.[1] I have no scholarly data to add to his meticulous work and no corrections to make in his elaborate mathematical tables; but I do question his value judgments, which he has made with no attempt whatever to view the poem in the context of other Middle English translations. Kurtz finds fault with Hoccleve for (1) omitting passages from the original Latin of Heinrich Suso merely because it was convenient, for prosodic reasons, for him to do so; (2) adding much material apparently for no other reason than to fill out a line or stanza; (3) using word pairs too frequently; and (4) giving us a poem twice the length of its original with nothing to justify the additional verbiage. As for the last point, I would suggest that any translation from Latin into English involves an increased number of words because of the differences in the languages. The idea expressed in one Latin verb, for example, must often be rendered by three, four, or even five English words. The word count of an English translation is also high, in comparison with a Latin original, because of the existence and frequent occurrence of articles. Regarding the use of word pairs, we have already observed that this is nothing peculiar to Hoccleve's verse but rather a common feature of medieval poetic. Medieval writers and their public looked on the device as a highly desirable means of ornamentation and expansion. As for Hoccleve's omissions and additions, it must be noted that in his day there were no established

[1] Benjamin P. Kurtz, "The Relation of Occleve's *Lerne to Dye* to Its Source," *PMLA*, XL (1925), 252-275.

rules that a translator was supposed to follow.[2] In fact the very word "translation" was used loosely by medieval writers; it could refer to a close rendering of an original, a free rendering, a compilation, or an epitome.

Most writers preferred free translations to literal ones, and they differed in their opinions on just what degree of liberty it was permissible to take. King Alfred tells us that he translated "sometimes word by word, and sometimes according to the sense."[3] John Trevisa, at the end of the fourteenth century, writes in a similar vein: "In some place I shall sette worde for worde & actyf for actyf & passyf for passyf arowe right as it stondeth without chaũgyng of the ordre of wordes. But in some place I must chaũge the ordre of wordes and sette actyf for passyf & ayenwarde / & in some place I must sette a reson for a worde / & telle what it meneth. But for all suche chaũgyng the menynge shall stande & not be chaunged."[4] John Capgrave, one of Hoccleve's contemporaries, would take further liberties: "This is þe preamble or elles þe prologe of Seynt Gilbertis lif, whech lyf I haue take on hand to translate out of Latyn rith as I fynde be-fore me, saue sum addicionis wil I put þertoo whech men of þat ordre haue told me, and eke othir þingis þat schul falle to my mynde in þe writyng whech be pertinent to þe mater."[5] The *Life of St. Gilbert* is in prose. *Metrical* translations were usually very free. No one thought it amiss for a poet to omit material in the original, to digress from it when he pleased, or to add lines which served primarily a rhetorical function. If many of the additions fell in the last lines of the rhyme-royal stanza, no one called attention to or complained about the poet's padding his work merely because of the exigencies of meter. After all, expansion was something to be expected in metrical translations, and just where the expansion should occur was a matter left to the discretion of the poet. Speaking in general terms one might say that a Middle English "translation" could follow or depart from its original to whatever extent pleased

[2] For a useful study of medieval concepts of translation see Flora Ross Amos, *Early Theories of Translation*, Columbia University Studies in English and Comparative Literature, LXVIII (New York, 1920).

[3] Preface to his translation of Pope Gregory's *Cura Pastoralis*, ed. Henry Sweet, E.E.T.S., O.S., No. 65 (London, 1871), p. 7.

[4] From Trevisa's Epistle to the Reader, prefixed to his translation of Ranulf Higden's *Policronicon* (Westmestre: Wynkn Theworde, 1495), fol. iii^{r}.

[5] *John Capgrave's Lives of St. Augustine and St. Gilbert of Sempringham*, ed. J. J. Munro, E.E.T.S., O.S., No. 140 (London, 1910), p. 62.

its maker. If Hoccleve's *Lerne to Dye* does not follow Suso's *Horologium* in a word-for-word fashion, the freer method of translation was certainly nothing extraordinary in medieval times. Kurtz's unwillingness to see the poem in the context of other medieval translations leads him to the curious position of both damning the work and pointing out that it contains not a few clever touches.

A good way to appreciate the variety of approaches a medieval translator might take in the handling of source material is to examine Hoccleve's *Letter of Cupid,* his *Regement of Princes,* and his two *Gesta* stories. In each case Hoccleve has used a different method of translation.

The *Letter of Cupid* is a rambling, amorphous work difficult to summarize. Cupid, the god of love, sends greetings to his earthly subjects and announces that many women have complained to him that they have been mistreated by men. The women say that men deceive them and then brag of their conquests to their fellow men. It is no wonder, Cupid muses, that women can be misled if Troy, one of the strongest cities of ancient times, was destroyed through deceit. Very often women are slandered by men whose advances they have refused. And sometimes *all* women are slandered by men who have found one or two to be unfaithful. Cupid notes that if a few women are wicked, it does not follow that all are so. The ladies complain bitterly that learned writers (like Ovid and Jean de Meun) delight in writing malicious books about them. Actually, Cupid observes, women would always be true if men were only faithful. Instead of being weak and inconstant, as men so often claim, women must on the contrary be strong if men have to resort to such base trickery to seduce them. The old, antifeminist argument that woman caused man to be expelled from the Garden of Eden is false. Men should remember that Jesus was born of a woman who was in no way "inconstant" or "variable." They should also remember that women stood by Jesus long after men had forsaken Him. Cupid says that he writes not to flatter women but rather to give them the courage to persevere in virtuous living. In conclusion, he orders his ministers to punish all evil men.

The *Letter* is less than three-fifths the length of its original, Christine de Pisan's *Epistre au Dieu d'Amours,* and on the whole it represents an extremely free handling of source material. Dryden would have called it an "imitation," that is, a type of translation in which "the translator (if now he has not lost that name) assumes the liberty, not only to vary from the words and sense, but to forsake them both as he sees occasion; and taking only some general hints from the original, to run division on the ground-work, as he pleases."[6] Although Hoccleve occasionally follows his source closely, he very often departs from it, rearranging material at will, omitting a great deal, and making several additions. *L'Epistre au Dieu d'Amours* is composed of 800 lines of decasyllabic couplets followed by 26 lines of tetrameter: Hoccleve's *Letter* has only 476 lines. That Hoccleve should want to abridge his source is remarkable in view of the fact that most writers of the age preferred expansion to abbreviation.

A comparison of Hoccleve's first stanza with the first seven lines of the *Epistre* shows that Hoccleve, even when following Christine, is more interested in giving the sense of the original than in making a literal translation:

Cupido / vn-to whos commandement
The gentil kynrede / of goddes on hy
And peple infernal been obedient,
And the mortel folk seruen bisyly;
Of goddesse Sitheree / sone oonly,
To alle tho / þat to our deitee
Been sogettes / greetynges senden we. [vv. 1-7]

Cupido, roy par la grace de lui,
Dieu des amans, sanz aide de nullui
Regnant en l'air du ciel trés reluisant,
Filz de Venus la deesse poissant,
Sire d'amours et de tous ses obgiez,
A tous nos vrais loiaulx servans subgiez,
Salut, Amour, Familiarité. [vv. 1-7]

Obviously some changes come about in this stanza and in all others because Hoccleve is converting from decasyllabic couplets to rhyme royal. The latter is a much more complicated metrical pattern; and thus, what Hoccleve can do with his source in any given stanza is pretty much dictated by the exigencies of the rhyme scheme and by the usual division of the material into units of seven lines. Only rarely does he use enjambment between stanzas.

Hoccleve's workmanship in stanzas ii-v is typical of his approach in much of the poem:

In general / we wole þat yee knowe
þat ladyes of honur and reuerence,
And othir gentil wommen, han I-sowe
Swich seed of conpleynte in our audience,

Savoir faisons en generalité
Qu'a nostre Court sont venues complaintes
Par devant nous et moult piteuses plaintes
De par toutes dames et damoiselles,

[6] Preface to the translation of Ovid's *Epistles*, included in *Essays of John Dryden*, ed. W. P. Ker, I (Oxford, 1900), 237.

Of men þat doon hem outrage & offense,
þat it oure eres greeueth for to heere,
So pitous is theffect of hir mateere,

And passyng alle londes / on this yle
That clept is Albioun / they moost conpleyne;
They seyn þat there is croppe and roote of gyle,
So can tho men dissimulen and feyne,
with standyng dropes in hire yen tweyne,
when þat hire herte / feelith no distresse,
To blynde wommen with hir doublenesse.

Hir wordes spoken been so sighyngly,
And with so pitous cheere and contenance,
That euery wight þat meeneth trewely
Deemeth / þat they in herte han swich greuance:
They seyn / so importable is hir penance,
þat, but hir lady / list to shewe hem grace,
They right anoon moot steruen in the place.

"A, lady myn" / they seyn / "I yow ensure,
Shewe me grace / & I shal euere be,
whyles my lyf may lasten & endure,
To yow as humble in euery degree
As possible is / and keepe al thyng secree,
As þat your seluen lykith þat I do,

Gentilz femmes, bourgoises et pucelles,
Et de toutes femmes generaument,
Nostre secours requerans humblement,
Ou, se ce non, du tout desheritées
De leur honneur seront et ahontées.
Si se plaingnent les dessusdittes dames
Des grans extors, des blasmes, des diffames,
Des traïsons, des oultrages trés griefs,
Des faussetez et de mains autres griefs,
Que chascun jour des desloiaulx reçoivent,
Qui les blasment, diffament et deçoivent.
Sur tous païs se complaignent de France,
Qui jadis fu leur escu et deffense,
Qui contre tous de tort les deffendoit,
Com il est droit, et si com faire doit
Noble païs ou gentillece regne.
Mais a present elles sont en ce regne,
Ou jadis tant estoient honnourées,
Plus qu'autre part des faulz deshonnourées,
Et meismement, dont plus griefment se deulent,
Des nobles gens qui plus garder les seulent.
Car a present sont pluseurs chevaliers
Et escuiers mains duis et coustumiers
D'elles traÿr par beaulx blandissemens.
Se se faignent estre loyaulx amans

And elles moot myn herte breste on two."

Et se cueuvrent de diverse faintise;
Si vont disant que griefment les atise
L'amour d'elles, qui leur cuer tient en serre,
Dont l'un se plaint, a l'autre le cuer serre,
L'autre pleure par semblant et souspire,
Et l'autre faint que trop griefment empire,
Par trop amer tout soit descoulouré
Et presque mort et tout alangoré,
Et jurent fort et promettent et mentent
Estre loiaulx, secrez, et puis s'en vantent.

The passage is a clear example of imitation, in Dryden's sense of the word. For one thing, Hoccleve very noticeably condenses his original, which is rich in detail. He is concerned with the complaints of only "ladyes" and "othir gentil wommen," whereas Christine speaks of the complaints "De par toutes dames et damoiselles, / Gentilz femmes, bourgoises et pucelles, / Et de toutes femmes generaument." He notes briefly that men do women "outrage & offense," instead of listing the various types of offenses, as does Christine (vv. 18-20). He considerably abridges Christine's remarks on the false lovers (vv. 28 ff.) and her account of their manifold deceits (vv. 36 ff.). There are other differences also. Some of the material in the original has been altogether omitted, such as the women's fear that they will lose all their honor if they are not aided (vv. 14-16) and the note that there were formerly noble men in the realm who defended women (vv. 24-27). An example of an outright change is Hoccleve's shifting of the action from France to "Albioun," or England, probably to catch the attention of his English public. As far as additions are concerned, one might note that Hoccleve's homely metaphors in lines 10-11 and in line 17 do not occur in Christine. More important, however, is his introduction in stanza v of direct discourse, which partly compensates for the loss of specificity caused by his earlier abbreviations. Instead of describing the various deceits which false lovers practice on their mistresses, he prefers to dramatize a specific situation. Although this particular passage is not especially arresting, it is nevertheless significant in view of Hoccleve's later work; for as Hoccleve developed his technique in the next twenty years, he became very adept in the handling of direct discourse.

A line-by-line comparison of the *Letter of Cupid* with Christine's *Epistre* shows that Hoccleve does not adhere to any single method of handling a source. In Chapter III I pointed out two instances in which he follows the French text very closely. Frequently, as in the illustration above, he condenses his source by abridging some passages and by omitting others altogether. Many more examples of omission could be pointed out. It is usually impossible to offer with certainty a reason that might have motivated Hoccleve to omit a particular passage in his source. About all one can say is that he never intended to follow his original in a line-by-line fashion and had evidently decided beforehand to make his work much shorter. Therefore he omitted whatever he pleased. In only one case is a noncapricious reason for an omission at all apparent. Hoccleve completely passes over Christine's long account (vv. 219 ff.) of two exemplary men, Hutin de Vermeilles and Otho de Grançon, probably because neither would have been known to an English public.

In several cases Hoccleve has actually expanded parallel material in his source. Stanzas vi-x, for example, a total of thirty-five lines, are based on lines 99-116 of the *Epistre* (only eighteen lines). The expansion is brought about partly through the introduction of a *sententia:*

> Ful hard is it to knowe a mannes herte,
> For outward may no man the truthe deeme,
> whan word out of his mowth / may ther noon sterte,
> But it sholde any wight by reson qweeme;
> So is it seid of herte / it wolde seeme.
>
> [vv. 36-40]

This is essentially the same idea Shakespeare's King Duncan expresses — more tersely, one might add — when he says, "There's no art / To find the mind's construction in the face" (*Macbeth* I.iv.11-12). The homely metaphor Hoccleve uses shortly afterwards is also not to be found in his source:

> And whan the man / the pot hath by the stele,
> And fully of hire hath possessioun,
> with þat womman he keepith nat to dele . . .
>
> [vv. 50-52]

On the other hand he omits some of Christine's graphic details, such as this one:

> . . . puis jurent corps et ames
> Comment du fait il leur est avenu
> Et que couché braz a braz y ont nu.
> [vv. 114-116]

But to compensate for the omission he heightens the pretentiousness of his style by the use of (1) an apostrophe:

> O feithful womman, ful of Innocence,
> Thow art betrayed by fals apparence!
> [vv. 41-42]

and (2) rhetorical questions:

> Is this a fair auant / is this honour,
> A man him-self to accuse & diffame?
> Now is it good, confesse him a traitour
> And brynge a womman to a sclaundrous name,
> And telle how he / hir body hath doon shame?
> [vv. 64-68]

Both these devices, like *sententiae*, are important aspects of his poetic technique. Another good example of expansion is the bawdy direct discourse of lines 99-112 (see Chapter II, Section 1). The three stanzas in praise of the Virgin (vv. 400-420) and the emotionally charged apostrophe to St. Margaret (vv. 421-427) are instances of downright additions rather than expansion of parallel material.

Hoccleve sometimes rearranges the material of his source; that is, he does not always follow Christine's verses in the order in which they were written. A good example is the analogy, in stanzas xii-xiii, which he draws between the betrayal of women and the fall of Troy and other realms. Just prior to this he was translating and expanding lines 99-116 of the *Epistre*. The analogy is based on Christine, but the corresponding French passage comes in a much later section of the poem — in lines 537-546. At stanza xv he returns to the earlier part of his source. Sometimes he rearranges the material of his source within a single stanza, as in the following instance:

> Ouyde, in his book callid Remedie
> Of loue / greet repreef of wommen writith;
> where-in I trowe / he dide greet folie,
> And euery wight / þat in swich cas delitith;
> A clerkes custume is whan he endytith
> Of wommen, be it prose / rym or vers,
> Seyn they be wikke / al knowe he the reuers.
> [vv. 204-210]

The lines criticizing Ovid at the beginning of the stanza follow, in a somewhat condensed form, this passage in the *Epistre:*

> Ovide en dit, en un livre qu'il fist,
> Assez de maulz, dont je tiens qu'il meffist,
> Qu'il appella le Remede d'amours,
> Ou leur met sus moult de villaines mours,
> Ordes, laides, pleines de villenie.
> [vv. 281-285]

Hoccleve's middle line is original; and here, his decision to break away from his source was probably dictated by the problem of working out the difficult *b*-rhyme. In the last three lines he skips back to an earlier section in Christine:

> Si se plaingnent les dessusdittes dames
> De pluseurs clers qui sus leur mettent blasmes,
> Dittiez en font, rimes, proses et vers,
> En diffamant leurs meurs par moz divers.
> [vv. 259-262]

His choice of the word "custume" (v. 208) is probably owing to Christine's *meurs,* even though Christine is referring to the *meurs* of women rather than of clerks. His *c*-rhyme was undoubtedly suggested by the rhyme *vers-divers* in the French.

In the last four stanzas of the poem Hoccleve sometimes follows Christine closely, but by abbreviation and omission he manages to reduce the number of lines from forty-one in the French to twenty-eight. The first of the four stanzas is a free rendering of lines 759-764 in Christine. In this case he has slightly expanded the parallel material. In the next stanza, however, he abbreviates his source and even finds room for an original apostrophe:

> O womman / þat of vertu art hostesse,
> Greet is thyn honur & thy worthynesse!
> [vv. 461-462]

In stanza lxvii he condenses the French by omitting Cupid's enumeration of the various types of ministers in his service. And in the final stanza he turns to a close rendering of the parallel material:

Fulfillid be it / cessyng al delay; Looke ther be noon excusacion! writen in their / the lusty monthe of May, In our Paleys / wher many a milion Of louers treewe / han habitacion,	Accompli soit sanz faire aucun delais. Donné en l'air, en nostre grant palais, Le jour de May la solempnée feste Ou les amans nous font mainte requeste,

The yeer of grace / ioieful & iocounde, M.CCCC. and secounde. [vv. 470-476]	L'An de grace Mil trois cens quatre vins Et dix et neuf, present dieux et divins. [vv. 795-800]

There is one important change here: the translator has moved the date forward from 1399 to 1402. Thus the *Letter of Cupid* is one poem in the Hoccleve canon that can be assigned a date with absolute certainty. The twenty-six lines of tetrasyllabic couplets which conclude Christine's poem do not appear in Hoccleve. The passage is merely a metrical catalogue of the various gods and goddesses who confirm Cupid's proclamation.

The *Letter of Cupid,* as I indicated in Chapter II, is a feminist poem. Various arguments against women are brought up so that they may be refuted. The last part of the work is quite eloquent in its espousal of the feminist cause. With all Hoccleve's rearrangement of the material in his source, one wishes that the *Letter* showed some degree of improvement over the French in organization. But such is not the case; both works are rambling and disjointed. With all Hoccleve's additions, expansions, and omissions one wishes that his work were of a higher artistic calibre than his source. Again such is not the case; both poems are typical, run-of-the-mill courtly poems. About all one can say is that the *Letter of Cupid* is shorter than *L'Epistre au Dieu d'Amours* and different from it in several respects — but not therefore better or worse. My principal intention in making the comparison has been to point out one method that Hoccleve used in handling source material.

The *Regement of Princes* represents another way in which Hoccleve handled his sources.[7] It is a compilation of passages selected mainly from three works — the *Secreta Secretorum,* Egidio Colonna's *De Regimine Principum,* and Jacobus de Cessolis' *Liber de Ludo Scacchorum* — and translated into English rhyme-royal stanzas (see Chapter II, Section 2). The following passage on *largesse,* taken from the *Secreta,* is typical of Hoccleve's workmanship in many parts of the poem:

And who doth othir wyse in his ȝeuyng, Largesses rule passith and excedith; He nouther worthi is þank ne preysyng, That to hym þat no nede hath, ȝiftes bedith.	Qui ergo dat aliter: peccat et regulam largitatis transcendit. quia qui largitur dona sua non

[7] See Friedrich Aster, *Das Verhältniss des altenglischen Gedichtes "De Regimine Principum" von Thomas Hoccleve zu seinen Quellen nebst einer Einleitung über Leben und Werke des Dichters* (diss. Leipzig, 1888).

Of verray folye also it procedith
To ȝeue the onworthi; for þat cost
All mysse dispendid is, for it is lost.

And he þat dispendith out of mesure
Shal tast a-none pouertes bitternesse;
ffoole largesse is ther-to a verray lure.
Of hem also he berith the lyknesse,
That on him self, as þe booke berith witnesse,
Victorie ȝeueth to his enemys;
And he þat so dispendith, is not wyse.
[vv. 4131-44]

indigentibus: Nullam acquirirt [*sic*] laudem et largiens sine tempore suo: ipse est sicut spargens aquas salsas super litus maris. et quicquid datur indignis perditur. et qui fundit ultra modum diuitias suas: ueniet cito ad amara littora paupertatis. et similatur illi qui super se dat suis victoriam inimicis [Aster, p. 18].

He expands his first line by translating *dat* (i.e., "gives") in a roundabout fashion: "doth . . . in his ȝeuyng." In the next line he completely omits the idea expressed in the Latin verb *peccat,* but he translates *transcendit* with one of his favorite devices, namely, a word pair: "passith and excedith." He leaves out an effective simile ("ipse est sicut spargens aquas salsas super litus maris") and substitutes for it a sententious remark: "Of verray folye also it procedith / To ȝeue the onworthi." In the next stanza he slightly changes one image ("ueniet cito ad amara littora paupertatis," i.e., "shall come quickly to the bitter shores of poverty," becomes "Shal tast a-none pouertes bitternesse"); he adds the idea of line 4140; he fills out another line with a conventional stopgap expression ("as þe booke berith witnesse"); and he rounds off the stanza with a *sententia* not in the Latin ("And he þat so dispendith, is not wyse").

Hoccleve's rather free handling of this extract from the *Secreta* is representative of his approach to the borrowed material in two of his principal sources, the *Secreta* and the *De Regimine Principum.* His renditions of *exempla* from Jacobus, on the other hand, are often fuller in detail and livelier in dramatic presentation than the original Latin. They show a marked degree of individuality on his part in the handling of his source. The anecdote about Julius Caesar and the knight under trial (vv. 3270-3304), to mention one example, is more than twice the length of the parallel Latin material (Aster, p. 44). Hoccleve expands the short clause "At ille ait" with descriptive details and repetition:

And vnto þat, þis knyght as blyue þus
On heighte wel, þat al þe peple it herde,

With manly cheere spak to Iulius,
His lorde, and in þis wise hym answerde: —
[vv. 3277-80]

He then expands the words of the knight — "O Caesar, te periclitante in bello Asiatico non vicarium quaesivi, sed pro te ego ipse pugnavi" — heightening the dramatic intensity of the situation:

"Han ye for-gote how scharp it wiþ yow ferde,
Whan ye were in þe werres of asie?
Maffeith! your lif stood þere in iupartie;

"And aduocat ne sente I non to yow,
But my-self put in prees, & for yow faght;
My woundes beren good witnesse y-now
That I sooth seye; and, lest ye leeue it naght,
I schal yow schewe what harme haue I caght,
The doute out of youre herte for to dryue."
[vv. 3281-89]

Aster has printed almost all the passages that Hoccleve utilizes in his three main sources together with the correponding English verses. Since the *Regement of Princes* is a compilation, Hoccleve arranges his source material *ad libitum;* he introduces the work with a long, partly autobiographical prologue; he inserts many original passages of social commentary; he includes several stanzas addressed directly to Prince Henry; in short, he comes up with a work quite different from any of his sources. The *Regement* is his only compilation.

The two *Gesta* poems represent still another way in which Hoccleve handled source material. In the *Tale of Jereslaus' Wife* he has followed his original, the Anglo-Latin *Gesta,* in a straightforward manner.[8] He has made no downright changes in the plot, no additions to it, and no rearrangement of the sequence of events.

The story divides into five well-defined parts. Part I (sts. i-ix) sets the stage. Emperor Jereslaus is introduced briefly (st. i), and then his wife, the heroine of the story and "a fair lady / to euery mannes ye" (v. 7), is introduced at somewhat greater length (st. ii).

[8] Brit. Mus. MS. Harl. 2270 is the most complete manuscript of the Anglo-Latin *Gesta* (see Chapter II, Section 6). All my quotations from the Story of Jereslaus' Wife follow Wallensköld's transcription in *Le Conte de la Femme Chaste Convoitée par Son Beau-frère,* Acta Societatis Scientiarum Fennicae, Vol. XXXIV, No. 1 (Helsingfors, 1907), pp. 111-116. Quotations from the Story of Jonathas and Felicia follow my own transcription, included in the first appendix to my unpublished doctoral dissertation, "Thomas Hoccleve: His Traditionalism and His Individuality: A Study in Fifteenth-Century English Poetic" (Duke, 1965).

In stanza iii the action gets under way. Having decided to make a pilgrimage to the Holy Land, Jereslaus makes arrangements for the government of the empire during his absence. Part II (sts. x-xxxviii) is devoted to the lady's difficulty with her brother-in-law, a wicked steward who tries to seduce her. When she refuses to be misled, he leaves her deep in the forest, half naked and hanging by her hair from the limb of a tree. Part III (sts. xxxix-lxii) relates how the lady is saved from death by a kind earl only to be tempted by another steward. When she refuses his overtures, he slips into the family bedchamber at night and murders the earl's daughter. With the skill of a Lady Macbeth he leaves the bloody knife in the hand of Jereslaus' wife, who is sleeping in the same bed with the victim, so that the guilt will appear hers. On the following morning the murder is discovered, and the grief-stricken earl, naturally assuming that the lady did the deed, drives her out of his realm. In Part IV (sts. lxiii-xcvii) the lady becomes involved with *two* wicked men. The first is a thief whom she saves from death at the gallows. He promises to be her faithful servant; but shortly afterwards he betrays her to a lecherous shipman, who entices her on board his ship and then suddenly orders the anchors to be raised. His amorous intentions are thwarted when the vessel is sunk in a storm and everyone is drowned except the lady and himself. Both cling to stray boards and are washed up on diverse shores, neither one knowing that the other is alive. In Part V (sts. xcviii-cxxxvi) the various strands of the story are brought together. The lady, now living in disguise in a nunnery, has acquired fame in the art of healing. All four men who have sinned against her — her brother-in-law, the earl's steward, the thief, and the shipman — come to her to be cured of grievous illnesses. She says she can help them only if they openly confess all their sins. The brother-in-law confesses in full after he makes Jereslaus, also present, promise not to punish him. Then, one by one, the other three briefly relate how they sinned against the virtuous lady. When all have publicly confessed, the lady cures them and reveals her identity to the entire company. Her husband Jereslaus is overjoyed. He leads her home to his palace, where they live for the rest of their lives "in ioie and hy honour" (v. 949).

From a dramatic standpoint the last part of the story is effective in both the original Latin and Hoccleve's version. The disguised lady says that she can cure the brother-in-law only if he confesses. When Jereslaus bids him do so, he makes a partial confession, omitting his brutal mistreatment of the empress. The lady then says that he must confess in full if he is to be cured. Jereslaus, who is of course ignorant of the reasons for his brother's reluctance to confess, becomes irritated and demands that he make a full shrift. At this dramatic point the brother makes Jereslaus promise that he will forgive him, whatever his sin might be. Jereslaus, ironically enough, promises his forgiveness. Now the brother is free to confess in full, and the climax of the story has arrived. The main reason for the effectiveness of this scene is that the situation is dramatically ironic in a double sense. The disguised lady, the brother, and we, the audience, are aware of past events of which Jereslaus and the rest of the company are ignorant. But we also know something which even the brother does not know, namely, that the disguised lady who can cure him is actually Jereslaus' wife, the very person he has wronged. A comparison of Hoccleve's version of this scene with the Anglo-Latin reveals that Hoccleve expands direct discourse and heightens its dramatic intensity. See, for example, his rendition of Jereslaus' curse:

"Thow cursid wrecche / thow demoniak!
þat our lord god / which for vs alle deide,
The strook of his vengeance / vp-on thee leide,
No wondir is / had y this beforn wist,
Thy body sholde han the grownd swept & kist;

"And ther-to eek / as sharpe punisshement
As þat dyuyse ther kowde any wight,
Thow sholdest han y-preeued by the sent;
But holde wole y / þat y thee haue hight."
[vv. 843-851]

"O pessime, vindicta Dei cecidit super te! Si istud ante sciuissem, moirti [i.e., morti] turpissime te condempnassem!" [Wallensköld, p. 115].

The comparison also reveals that Hoccleve inserts a digression just after the brother's full confession (vv. 820 ff.). In it he meditates for three stanzas on Jereslaus' emotional reaction to the events of the story.

Hoccleve often interrupts the story with personal intrusions and brief digressions. The first significant intrusion comes at stanza ix, its purpose being to mark the end of Part I:

The sorwe of herte / and cheer of heuynesse
Which this good lady at his departynge
Made / the book nat can telle or expresse;
Wherfore / of þat haue I no knowlechynge;
Eek kepe I nat / the belle of sorwe out rynge,
Thogh þat I kneew wel euery circumstance
Of hir wo / & hir heuy contenance.
[vv. 57-63]

At stanza xxv the action momentarily stops as the poet apostrophizes the lady ("O noble lady / symple and Innocent," etc.) and comments briefly on the trouble to ensue. A pause just before a climactic scene contributes to the building up of suspense; it is the lull before the storm. In this case the painful scene Hoccleve is postponing is the one wherein the brother-in-law tries to seduce the lady and upon failing leaves her to die in the forest. The scene is of such importance that Hoccleve heightens the suspense by pausing once more, at stanza xxviii, this time to note the difference in social customs between his own day and ancient times. He closes Part II in stanzas xxxvi-xxxviii with an emotionally charged apostrophe to the wicked brother-in-law. A few lines of his impassioned rhetoric show that he has no intention of telling his story objectively:

O false lyer / o thow cofre and cheste
Of vnclennesse / o stynkynge Aduoutour
In wil, seye I / and willy to inceste;
O false man to god / and thow traitour
To thy lord and brothir, the Emperour;
O enemy to wyfly chastitee,
And in thy wirkes ful of crueltee;

O cursid feendly wrecche / why hast thow
Deceyued & betrayed Innocence?
[vv. 246-254]

At two points in the story a digression comes *after* the action has built up to a climax. One scene in question occurs in Part III. The countess has just awakened from sleep and discovered that her daughter has been murdered. Her speech broken by anger and grief, she demands that her lord immediately execute the lady, whom she believes guilty. When the action has reached this peak of excitement, Hoccleve digresses for two stanzas to observe that the countess cannot be blamed since she was acting in accordance with her motherly instinct. He ends the digression with a brief, humorous reference to his own marital life (vv. 394-399). Then the story is taken up again, the climax being resolved not by the lady's execution, but by her perpetual banishment from the earl's domain. Another digression of this type comes after the story's most dramatic moment — after the repentant brother-in-law has finally told the assembled company how he mistreated the virtuous lady (see above). The purpose of these digressions is to give the reader or listener a chance to relax his attention for a moment and reflect on what has passed before the action moves forward.

Sometimes, in an apostrophe, Hoccleve gives his audience a hint of what is to follow. Such a passage marks the end of Part III:

> O Emperice / our lord god gye thee,
> ffor yit thee folwith more aduersitee.
> [vv. 433-434]

A more optimistic foreshadowing interrupts the action of Part IV, shortly before the lady boards the vessel to buy merchandise from the lecherous shipman:

> O / Emperice / god the gye and lede!
> Thow haast, or this, had trouble greet & drede,
> And yit a sharp storm is vn-to thee shape;
> But, thankid be god / al thow shalt eschape.
> [vv. 578-581]

Other digressions could be pointed out also.

To sum up, Hoccleve's digressions in the *Tale of Jereslaus' Wife* are a very noticeable feature of his work in comparison with the original Latin. He has not always superimposed them onto the story haphazardly. Some foreshadow events to come, others contribute to the development of suspense, and still others round off major divisions of the poem. Hoccleve's digressive passages are about the only instances in which the *Tale of Jereslaus' Wife* differs markedly from the Anglo-Latin original, which Hoccleve, not adhering to his earlier methods of handling source material, has translated in its entirety.

Another aspect of Hoccleve's workmanship in contrast with the original Latin is his use of transitional expressions. Even the most obtuse reader or listener could hardly misunderstand the narrative development of the *Tale of Jereslaus' Wife*. A typical transition comes at the beginning of stanza iii: "Now in my tale foorth wole I proceede." Stanza ii had been devoted to a description of the virtues of the heroine. Another example is the transition following the digression at the end of Part II:

> Wherfore to my tale wole I go,
> Of this lady / and foorth tell of hir wo.
> [vv. 265-266]

Most of the transitions mark the poet's return to the story after a passage of digressive material. At the end of the digression on motherly instinct in Part III (see above), Hoccleve picks up the story again with a transitional phrase of only two words: "Now foorth" (v. 400). After he has expounded on woman's constancy, he returns to the narrative with the words "Let al this passe" — an expression which some 200 years later was to be a favorite of the Wife in Dekker's *Shoemakers' Holiday.* A list of transitional expressions used in similar positions would include "Now to purpos" (v. 582); "Now to the Emperour, torne wole y" (v. 729); "Now to my purpos" (v. 841); and "No force of þat / my tale I now thus eende" (v. 946). Between Parts IV and V occur these lines:

> Of this shipman / speke y no more as now;
> But this lady / vn-to a Nonnerie
> þat was but there fast by / hir drow . . .
> [vv. 680-682]

This transition differs from the ones just mentioned in that it does not follow a digressive passage. It resembles rather the type of thing found very often in *Emare,* one of the popular tail-rhyme romances and an analogue of Hoccleve's *Gesta* poem.[9] None of the transitional expressions in the *Tale of Jereslaus' Wife* can be found in the original Latin. Like the conventional minstrel tags and stopgap expressions discussed earlier, they are usually associated with popular verse, but they can also be found occasionally in the work of literary artists such as Chaucer and Gower.

Much the same can be said about Hoccleve's handling of source material in the *Tale of Jonathas* as has already been said regarding *Jereslaus' Wife.* It too can be divided into five parts. The first part begins actually at stanza xiii in Furnivall's edition, the first twelve stanzas comprising a prologue in which Hoccleve records how he was persuaded by a friend to translate another *Gesta* tale.

In Part I (sts. xiii-xxii) a dying father divides his estate among his three sons. The third son, Jonathas, has been given a ring, a brooch, and a cloth, all of which have magical properties. He takes the ring with him when he leaves home to go to the university. Part II (sts. xxiii-xxxix) concerns Jonathas' relations with his false mistress, Fellicula, his loss of the ring, and his return to his mother. The same pattern is repeated in Part III (sts. xl-lii) as Jonathas loses his second gift, the magic brooch. In like fashion he loses the flying carpet in Part IV (sts. liii-lxiii), but this time he cannot return so easily to his mother, since Fellicula has treacherously left him stranded at the edge of the world. Part V (sts. lxiv-xcvi) is concerned with Jonathas' slow journey back to civilization and his revenge on Fellicula. At the very end he returns with the three leg-

[9] Ed. Edith Rickert, E.E.T.S., E.S., No. 99 (London, 1906 [issued in 1908]). See vv. 70-72, 310-312, 742-744, 946-948.

acies home to his mother, and there he lives "in ioie and in prosperitee" until his "dyynge day."

The story is so designed that all the action evolves to Jonathas' disadvantage until Part V. At the beginning of Part V he walks through a lake of hot water which burns the flesh from his feet, and he eats a fruit which turns him at once into a leper. At this point he is utterly dejected, exclaiming:

. . . "Cursid be þat day þat I was born / and tyme and hour also þat my modir conceyued me / for ay Now am I lost / allas and weleaway!" [vv. 471-474]	"Heu, michi! Quid faciam vel ubi fugiam penitus ignoro. Omnia ista mala bene merui quia totum concilium meum mulieri expandidi."

Hoccleve's free rendition of the brief complaint is more intense than the Latin. All seems to be lost; but these words of Jonathas mark the turning point of the story, and from this moment on, things begin gradually to work in his favor. If his revenge on Fellicula seems too brutal (he poisons her with the scalding water and the tainted fruit), one must remember that she, according to the moralization, represents the flesh, and therefore she must be overcome if Jonathas (man) is to re-enter his native land (the kingdom of heaven).

In the *Tale of Jonathas* Hoccleve has cut all digressive material to a minimum. After the mother's lament on the death of her husband in Part I, he digresses briefly on widows (vv. 141-146). A few lines later he makes a humorous aside during his account of Jonathas' courtship:

And he a pistle rowned in hire ere:
Nat woot y what / for y ne cam nat there.
[vv. 167-168]

The longest digressive passage is his apostrophe to Jonathas, marking the end of Part IV. In it he tells us that despite Jonathas' hard luck, things will turn out in the end for the best. Another digression occurs in Part V, just after the action has reached a climax. As in *Jereslaus' Wife,* the climax involves the confession of someone anxious to be rid of a grievous illness. When Fellicula makes her confession, however, she does so not with a contrite heart, but solely with the idea of being cured. Hoccleve then makes a brief digression on the etymology of Fellicula's name:

. . . O Fellicula, thee call
Wel may y so / for of the bittir gall
Thow takist the begynnynge of thy name,
Thow roote of malice / and mirour of shame!
[vv. 634-637]

Fel in Latin means "the gall, the gall-bladder" and in a figurative sense "bitterness" or "anger." Sometimes the word means "the venom of a serpent," and this meaning is reminiscent of Hoccleve's earlier reference to Fellicula as "this serpentyn womman" (v. 572). These are virtually all the digressive passages in the *Tale of Jonathas,* which, from the viewpoint of structure, is more concise and tightly knit together than *Jereslaus' Wife.*

In several places I have observed that Hoccleve shows proficiency in the handling of direct discourse. In no poem is this more evident than in the *Tale of Jonathas.* The following dialogue, quoted side by side with the parallel source material, shows clearly the nature of his workmanship. The scene is a bedchamber. Fellicula is cleverly trying to persuade Jonathas to tell her the source of his unlimited wealth:

"O reuerent sire / vn-to whom," quod shee, "Obeye y wole ay with hertes humblesse, Syn / þat yee han had my virginitee, yow y byseeche, of your hy gentillesse, Tellith me whens comth the good & richesse That yee with feesten folke / and han no stoor, By aght y see can / ne gold ne tresor."	"Domine mi reverende, virginitatem meam habuisti et totaliter quamdiu vixero ad vestram voluntatem me paratam invenietis. Rogo te ut unam petitionem concedas michi: Dic michi si placiet quomodo tot bona adquiris et diversa convivia facis et nec thesaurum vel pecunias vidi te habere."
"If y telle it," quod he / "par auenture Thow wilt deskeuere it / & out it publisshe: Swich is wommannes inconstant nature, They can nat keepe conseil worth a risshe; Bettre is, my tonge keepe / than to wisshe þat y had kept cloos þat is goon at large, And repentance is thyng þat y moot charge."	At ille: "Si forte veritatem tibi propalavero concilium meum revelabis."
"Nay, goode sire / haldith me nat suspect; Doutith nothyng; y can be right secree. wel worthy were it me to been abiect ffrom all good conpaignie / if y," quod shee, "Vn-to yow sholde so mis take me; Beeth nat adrad your Conseil me to shewe."	At illa: "Absit hoc me quod tale facinus contra vos perpetrarem."
"wel," seide he / "thus it is, at wordes fewe:	At ille:

"My fadir, the ryng which þat thow maist see
On my fyngir / me at his dyyng day
Byqweeth / which this vertu & propretee
hath / þat the loue of men, he shal haue ay
þat werith it / and ther shal be no nay,
Of what thyng þat him lykith axe & craue,
But with good wil / he shal as blyue it haue

"Pater meus reliquit istum anulum quem videre poteris in digito meo; unde talem virtutem habet quod quicumque illum portaverit amorem omnium habebit. Et omnes ideo tantum me diligunt quod quicquid ab eis peto michi dant et concedunt."

"Thurgh þat rynges vertuous excellence:
Thus am y ryche, and haue euere ynow."
"Now, sire, yit a word, by your licence,
Suffrith me for to seye and speke now;
Is it wysdam / as þat it seemeth yow,
were it on your fyngir continuelly?"
"what woldest thow mene," quod he, "ther-by?

At illa: "Domine mi reverende, quare istud prius non revelasti propter periculum quod potest accidere?"
Ait Jonathas:

"What peril ther-of mighte ther befall?"
"Right greet," quod she / "as yee in conpaignye
walke often / fro your fyngir mighte it fall,
Or plukkid of been in a ragerie,
And so be lost / and þat were folie.
Take it me / let me been of it wardeyn;
ffor as my lyf, keepe it wole y certeyn."

"Quod periculum potest accidere?" At illa: "Sepius pergis in civitatibus variis et a casu anulum perdere possitis, et esset tale iocale perdere periculum. Ideo, karissime, trade michi anulum et ego sicut vitam meam eum custodiam."

In the first stanza Hoccleve follows his source very closely, but he adds a few touches that contribute to his characterization of Fellicula. He emphasizes her unctuous cajolery with phrases (not in the Latin) such as "with hertes humblesse" (v. 184) and "of your hy gentillesse" (v. 186). The verb "byseeche" (v. 186) is stronger than the Latin *Dic*. "O reuerent sire" (v. 183) is, of course, a literal translation of "Domine mi reverende." Jonathas' words in the first two lines of the next stanza are a close translation of the Latin. The rest of the stanza, however, is Hoccleve's invention. It consists of a humorous proverbial statement (vv. 192-193) followed by a *sententia* (vv. 194-196). In lines 190-191 Hoccleve does not translate the Latin noun *concilium* (he uses instead the pronoun "it" to refer to Fellicula's previous remark), but in his added proverbial statement he chooses the word "conseil" obviously because of the Latin.

The additional verbiage in the third stanza — "Nay, goode sire / haldith me nat suspect," etc. — makes Fellicula's protestation that she can keep a secret more lifelike and therefore more convincing than the original Latin. The colloquial beginning of Jonathas' revelation — "wel . . . thus it is, at wordes fewe" (v. 203) — is a realistic touch. The first part of the fourth stanza (Jonathas is speaking) follows the Latin closely, but lines 208-212 reveal that Hoccleve has again expanded his source. Here, however, the additional verbiage is of little consequence. In the fifth stanza Fellicula's remarks follow the Latin to some extent, but added phrases such as "by your licence" (v. 213) and "as þat it seemeth yow" (v. 215) emphasize once again her clever way of wheedling Jonathas into giving her the ring. Jonathas' question at the end of the fifth stanza does not appear in the Latin, and it, added to the next question (which *is* in the Latin), makes his discourse seem realistic. The first words of Fellicula's reply — "Right greet" (v. 219) — contribute somewhat to the naturalness of the English dialogue. So also does her suggestion (not in the Latin) that Jonathas' ring might be plucked from his finger "in a ragerie" (v. 221). All six stanzas display a dialogue more realistic, more lifelike, and more convincing than the corresponding Latin. The passage is a representative example of Hoccleve's individuality in "translating" direct discourse.

In all his many works, autobiographical and otherwise, Hoccleve says practically nothing about his own feelings regarding the handling of source material. One *apparent* exception occurs in the *Dialogue with a Friend.* The Friend has just criticized Hoccleve for writing disparagingly of women in the *Letter of Cupid.* Hoccleve replies:

> "ffreend / doutelees sumwhat ther is ther-in
> þat sowneth but right smal to hir honour;
> But as to þat / now, for your fadir kyn,
> Considereth / ther-of / was I noon Auctour;
> I nas in þat cas / but a reportour
> Of folkes tales / as they seide / I wroot:
> I nat affermed it on hem / god woot!
>
> "Who so þat shal reherce a mannes sawe,
> As þat he seith / moot he seyn & nat varie,
> ffor, and he do / he dooth ageyn the lawe
> Of trouthe / he may tho wordes nat contrarie."
> [vv. 757-767]

In the first half of the *Letter* Hoccleve (following Christine) does recount some of the antifeminist ideas of frustrated lovers and malicious intellectuals; and in the passage above he expresses the idea that he, as a reporter of other folks' tales, was compelled to record the antifeminist sentiments as faithfully as possible. He suggests that a writer ought to be true to his source and to render the material contained therein without any variance — even though he himself might be opposed to much of it. The implication is that a translator cannot be held responsible for the words and opinions he translates.

Is this really an important expression on Hoccleve's part of his artistic principles? Probably not. In the final analysis it is more reminiscent of similar passages in Chaucer[10] and Lydgate[11] — passages obviously written with tongue in cheek — than indicative of any principles Hoccleve held regarding the handling of source material. The two *Gesta* poems are the only "translations" wherein he follows his source at all faithfully. In the *Regement of Princes* and the *Letter of Cupid* he shows no qualms about varying from his originals in almost every conceivable way. The only safe generalization which can be made about Hoccleve's ideas on "translation" — and this is based on his practice rather than his personal comments — is that Hoccleve looked on a Latin or French source as something an English "translator" could utilize in whatever way he pleased.

To sum up, Hoccleve's handling of source material is best understood and appreciated in the context of other Middle English literature. If his translations seem free by modern standards, one must remember that there was no uniformity of opinion in the Middle Ages regarding a writer's use of borrowed material. Hoccleve's workmanship is, on the whole, typical of his age. But in one respect, his handling of direct discourse taken from Latin and French sources, he shows individuality and unusual skill. His lively, realistic direct discourse is one of his most important achievements.

[10] General Prologue to the *Canterbury Tales* (A 725 ff.) and the Miller's Prologue (A 3167 ff.).

[11] See Chapter II, Section 7.

CHAPTER V

METER

If one had to pick the aspect of Hoccleve's poetic technique that has most caused his reputation to fall into low repute, it would certainly be his meter — or rather his meter as understood by late nineteenth- and early twentieth-century critics. Hoccleve has been severely criticized by almost everyone for, as he himself once put it, "meetrynge amis." In the most comprehensive nineteenth-century study of English metric Jakob Schipper calls particular attention to what he believes to be Hoccleve's frequent use of "schwebende Betonung," that is, the placing of a verse accent on words or syllables normally unstressed.[1] Furnivall points out the same supposed fault: "Hoccleve's metre is poor. So long as he can count ten syllables by his fingers, he is content. . . . He constantly thwarts the natural run of his line by putting stress on a word that shouldn't bear it, or using a strong syllable for a weak one."[2] Franz Bock says precisely the same thing in the only full-length study of Hoccleve's meter.[3] So also does George Saintsbury, who eloquently reiterates all previous disparaging remarks on the verse of Hoccleve and Lydgate and concludes "that the whole thing is prosaic, hobbling, broken-backed doggerel."[4] Saintsbury wrote his *History of English Prosody* in the first decade of this century. With one notable exception, to be considered below, subse-

[1] *Englische Metrik,* I (Bonn, 1881), 488-489.

[2] Hoccleve's *Minor Poems,* p. xli. As usual, all my quotations follow Furnivall's and Gollancz's texts; but in this chapter I have called attention to editorial emendations wherever they might have an effect on the meter.

[3] *Metrische Studien zu Thomas Hoccleves Werken* (diss. Munich, 1900), p. iv.

[4] *A History of English Prosody from the Twelfth Century to the Present Day,* I (London, 1906), 234.

quent writers who discuss Hoccleve's meter have simply echoed Saintsbury's opinions.

A re-examination of the earlier studies of Hoccleve's meter with careful attention to the many supposed examples of "thwarted stress" yields surprising results. Let us consider for a moment the following line from the *Letter of Cupid:*

Ne to cause hem pryde or elacioun
[v. 452]

If critics such as Schipper, Furnivall, Bock, or Saintsbury were to scan this line, they would make it conform to a regular line of iambic pentameter. Even though the verse accents might come in awkward places and reveal the most objectionable thwarted stress conceivable, the line would be forced into this pattern:

U / U / U / U / U /
Ne to | cause hem | pryde or | ela|cioun

The natural outcome of such a scansion is that Hoccleve is damned as a metrist because he took no heed "nouther of shorte nor longe," to borrow an often quoted expression from Lydgate. Hoccleve is accused of putting heavy accents on words and syllables which never have stress in normal speech and of hastily passing over words and syllables which in all reason should receive stress. Of course one does not have to be a professional student of English meter to recognize that this same line might be scanned in another way. Anyone not having a preconceived notion about the nature of medieval versification can readily see that the following scansion is not only possible but reasonable withal:

/ U / U / U U / U /
Ne | to cause | hem pryde | or ela|cioun

This scansion does away with all supposed instances of thwarted stress. The line is headless (or "acephalous"), to be sure, but this is nothing unusual in Middle English poetry. Chaucer himself wrote many headless lines.

The type of scansion that produces thwarted stress in the above-cited line from the *Letter of Cupid* goes hand in hand with a curious theory of meter propounded by Albert H. Licklider in his *Chapters on the Metric of the Chaucerian Tradition* (Baltimore, 1910). Licklider assumes initially that the stresses of English verse are fixed. "These remain intact," he writes, "for only then can the integrity of the real metrical unit, the line, be preserved. Variety is obtained, not by sacrificing the structure of the metrical unit, the line, but by clever manipulation of its stresses *without changing their positions:* by discreet syllabic combinations within the articulations of the line, *again without disturbing the normal recurrence of the stresses*" (p. 40; italics mine). This basic assumption leads the author to fantastic ways of scanning fifteenth-century verse. He suggests, for example, a thoroughly rigidified scansion of these lines from Lydgate's *Temple of Glass:*[5]

U / U / U / U / U /
And seid | Allas | what þing | mai | þis be
[v. 567]

U / U / U / U / U /
Siþ noon | but she | may | þi sor|es sound
[v. 1200]

Licklider's division of *mai* into two syllables with a stress on the second is unworthy of serious consideration. Most people would consider *mai* a monosyllabic word having one heavy stress. Thus both the lines above are typical examples of the broken-backed line so often associated with Lydgate's verse (see below).

Licklider calls the peculiar theory of meter which he advocates the "rhythm-doctrine." By this he means "the reading of poetry as poetry and not as prose; with due regard to the demands of the three threads of rhythm, — word-accent, rhetorical stress, and verse-ictus. . . . When this verse-accent or ictus stands in conflict with word-accent, it is marked by *increased duration of the vocalic element under the ictus,* attended, in the majority of cases, but not necessarily, by *increase also of pitch.* The result is the addition to a weak syllable of length and of pitch-accent, which mark the ictus as adequately as an intensified primary stress would do" (p. 119). These remarks lie behind his discussion of "arsis-thesis variation," that is, the placing of the same word or syllable sometimes in the arsis and at other times in the thesis, in either the same line or consecutive lines. He shows many examples of arsis-thesis variation in the poetry of Hoccleve, whom he considers the chief representative of the device in the post-Chaucerian period (pp. 202-212).

Licklider's so-called rhythm-doctrine — a theory which does not recognize metrical inversion and substitution — has not been widely accepted. Eleanor Prescott Hammond, to mention one opponent, rejects it altogether: "It is obvious that the single line shows, in both modern and medieval English verse, a frequent coincidence of

[5] Ed. Josef Schick, E.E.T.S., E.S., No. 60 (London, 1891).

theoretic stress with unimportant syllable; but instead of explaining this coincidence, in any poet, as a heightening of word-value by the impact of immutable stress, I shall treat the line and the paragraph as plastic, subject at every moment to the shaping hand of the poet; I shall recognize . . . the 'perpetual conflict' of the verse-norm and of language-freedom as the living foundation of English verse."[6] She then scans a line from Milton — "Deep malice to conceal, coucht with revenge" — and explains the meter in terms of "the poet's shift of word-weight within the verse; a heavy first foot, a light second, a reversed fourth, challenge the reader's ear by their divergence from standard as regards the massing of stress, while the total weight of the line remains standard." Miss Hammond's analysis represents what I would call a common-sense approach to meter, that is, one that recognizes metrical inversion and substitution. This, of course, is essentially the same view of pentameter line structure advocated by Cleanth Brooks and Robert Penn Warren in *Understanding Poetry* (New York, 1938) and by James R. Kreuzer in *Elements of Poetry* (New York, 1955). Yet, strangely enough, a view of English metric much like that of Licklider's apparently lies behind all the disparaging evaluations of Hoccleve's meter. My purpose in this chapter is to show that Hoccleve's line structure, if analyzed in terms of more recent ideas on meter, is by no means so crude as many writers have thought.

A survey of the critical opinion during the last seventy-five years regarding Lydgate's versification suggests that the last word has not been said about Hoccleve. Many of the earlier critics, such as Schipper and Saintsbury, damned Lydgate as a metrist along with Hoccleve, and their opinions are reflected to some extent in twentieth-century literary histories. There is another school of thought, however, which attempts to show that in matters of versification Lydgate was a highly skilled craftsman. The movement began with Josef Schick's introduction to his edition of the *Temple of Glass* (1891). Using a discussion in Schipper's *Englische Metrik* as a point of departure, Schick divided Lydgate's five-beat iambic lines into five different types:

A. The regular type, composed of five iambs, to which an extra syllable may sometimes be added at the end. There is usually a caesura after the second foot.

[6] *English Verse Between Chaucer and Surrey* (Durham, N.C., 1927), p. 84.

U / U / U / U / U /
For thouȝt, | constreint, || and greu|ous heu|inesse
[*Temple of Glass,* v. 1]

B. Lines similar to the preceding type, but containing an extra light syllable before the caesura.

U / U /U U / U / U /
I fond | a wiket, || and en|trid in | as fast
[*Ibid.,* v. 39]

C. The type associated primarily with Lydgate in which an unstressed syllable is missing just after the caesura, with the result that two heavy syllables come together. This is the so-called broken-backed line.

U / U / / U / U /
Siþ noon | but she || may | þi sor|es sound
[*Ibid.,* v. 1200]

D. The headless (or acephalous) line.

/ U / U / U / U /
Vn|to hir || & to | hir ex|cellence
[*Ibid.,* v. 1396]

E. Lines with a trisyllabic first measure.

U U / U / U / U / U /
That was feiþ|ful found, || til hem | depart|id deþe
[*Ibid.,* v. 781]

All subsequent editors of Lydgate have more or less accepted this fivefold classification. Schick did not claim that Lydgate's versification was smoother than Chaucer's, but he observed in conclusion that "if the metre of Lydgate is 'halting,' there is, as a rule, method in this halting" (p. lxiii).

Most twentieth-century editors of Lydgate speak highly of his versification. In the introduction to his edition of *Reson and Sensuallyte* Ernst Sieper praises the metrical qualities of the work.[7] Henry Bergen, editor of the *Troy Book,* suggests that the "violent prejudice" against Lydgate's meter may have arisen from inferior printed editions. He notes that Lydgate's free handling of unstressed syllables represents a return "from Chaucer's and Gower's syllabic purism" to native traditions in verse.[8] Henry Noble MacCracken does not find the broken-backed line objectionable. "I have tried

[7] Lydgate's *Reson and Sensuallyte,* Pt. 1, E.E.T.S., E.S., No. 84 (London, 1901), p. 18.

[8] Lydgate's *Troy Book,* Pt. 1, E.E.T.S., E.S., No. 97 (London, 1906), pp. xvi-xvii.

reading *Troy Book* aloud," he writes, "and have come to agree with its editor that it is a pleasant variation of the line."[9] In the temporary preface to the *Siege of Thebes* Axel Erdmann remarks that the fashionable denomination of the poem "as a specimen of unusually bad metre" is without foundation.[10] Bergen sums up his feelings about Lydgate's verse in his edition of the *Fall of Princes:* ". . . Lydgate's decasyllabic lines are far better, in the sense of being more capably written from a purely metrical point of view, than some of his modern critics, who evidently had no proper facilities for studying his work, were able to discover."[11] Joseph A. Lauritis has recently pointed out that scholars who have actually edited a significant poem by Lydgate all agree that he was a very capable metrist, while the nonediting critics form "a solid block in disagreement."[12] Father Lauritis finds that the *Life of Our Lady* scans easily and smoothly according to Schick's fivefold classification of pentameter lines. He concludes that as a metrist Lydgate "seems to have few equals."

James G. Southworth does not praise Lydgate so highly as does Father Lauritis, but he writes that "it is a great injustice to [Lydgate] to think that he could not write correct verse."[13] Southworth's remarks are a part of his argument that Chaucer and his followers did not write iambic decasyllabic verse at all. The theory of iambic decasyllables, he believes, is something that was foisted upon students by nineteenth-century scholars such as Child, Schipper, ten Brink, and Skeat. Under the influence of the earlier scholars, modern editors of Chaucer and his followers have manufactured texts that do scan as decasyllabic verse. Yet no single manuscript indicates that medieval English poets thought in terms of iambic decasyllables. Southworth believes that the medieval poets wrote what he calls

[9] Lydgate's *Minor Poems*, Pt. 1, E.E.T.S., E.S., No. 107 (London, 1911 [for 1910]), p. viii, n. 1. MacCracken says furthermore that "Lydgate is always smooth" (p. xxxv).

[10] Lydgate's *Siege of Thebes*, Pt. 1, E.E.T.S., E.S., No. 108 (London, 1911), pp. vii-viii.

[11] Lydgate's *Fall of Princes*, I (Washington, 1923), xxviii.

[12] Lydgate's *Life of Our Lady*, ed. Joseph A. Lauritis, Ralph A. Klinefelter, and Vernon F. Gallagher (Pittsburgh, 1961), pp. 191-195.

[13] *Verses of Cadence: An Introduction to the Prosody of Chaucer and His Followers* (Oxford, 1954), p. 78. What follows in my paragraph is largely a summary of important points that Southworth makes. See also his *The Prosody of Chaucer and His Followers: Supplementary Chapters to "Verses of Cadence"* (Oxford, 1962), pp. 73-76 *et passim*; and "Chaucer: A Plea for a Reliable Text," *College English*, XXVI (1964), 173-179.

"verses of cadence." Very often their lines contain five primary stresses (as in normal pentameter), but sometimes they contain six stresses or only four. Southworth's point, then, is that fourteenth- and fifteenth-century verse should be read "rhythmically" (i.e., according to the rhythms of medieval speech) instead of "metrically"; for only in this way does it make sense esthetically. It is unfortunate, he observes, that most Middle English verse has been made to fit an iambic decasyllabic pattern by modern editors — editors who have disregarded the importance of the virgule in manuscripts, added final *e*'s *ad libitum,* and made other emendations based on unwarrantable theories. As far as Hoccleve is concerned, Southworth shows, in a brief discussion, that his poetry reads very well "rhythmically." He questions the commonly held notion that Hoccleve was unable to understand Chaucer's rhythm and thus wrote verse characterized by thwarted stress.

In the next few pages I shall re-examine several lines from Hoccleve which earlier scholars have pointed to as glaring instances of thwarted stress. I contend that there is no thwarted stress at all (1) if the lines are scanned according to Brooks and Warren's method of scansion, that is, a method that recognizes metrical substitution and inversion; or (2) if they are scanned according to the fivefold classification of pentameter lines used by Schick and others with respect to Lydgate; or (3) if they are read "rhythmically," that is, as "verses of cadence," according to the method advocated by Southworth.

Furnivall, we have seen earlier, denies Hoccleve any degree of metrical competence whatsoever. In the prefatory material to his edition of Hoccleve's *Minor Poems* (p. xli) he points out three lines in the *Dialogue with a Friend* which he believes are examples of thwarted stress. I give the lines with *his* stress marks:

      /
ffûl many á man / for to taken heede
[v. 605]

                                 /
Now, good freend / shoue at thé cart, I yow preye
[v. 617]

              /   /   /
Right so / let ít be bý wrytýnge amendid
[v. 700]

In the first example there is no reason to suppose that Hoccleve intended the indefinite article to be accented. The line scans very easily as a C-type, to borrow Schick's classification, with the substitution of an anapest in the second foot:

U / UU / / U / U /
fful man|y a man | for | to tak|en heede

The pattern of stresses is perhaps the same if the line is read as a verse of cadence:[14]

U / UU / / U / U /
♪ | ♪ ♪♪ | ♩. | ♩ ♪ | ♩ ♪ | ♩
fful many a man / for to taken heede

One might note, however, that the following readings are also possible:

U / UU / U U / U /
♪ | ♪ ♪ ♪ | ♩ ♪ ♪ | ♩ ♪ | ♩
fful many a man / for to taken heede

/ / UU / U U / U /
| ♪. | ♪ ♪ ♪ | ♩ ♪ ♪ | ♩ ♪ | ♩
fful many a man / for to taken heede

/ / UU / / U / U /
| ♪. | ♪ ♪ ♪ | ♩. | ♩ ♪ | ♩ ♪ | ♩
fful many a man / for to taken heede

Furnivall's second example can be scanned more reasonably as a headless line, with inversion in the third foot and substitution in the fifth:

/ U / / U U / U U /
Now, | good freend | shoue at | the cart, | I yow preye

The pattern of stresses is the same if the line is read rhythmically:

/ U / / U U / U U /
| ♪. ♪. | ♩. | ♪ ♪ ♪ | ♪ ♪ ♪ | ♩
Now, good freend / shoue at the cart, I yow preye

As for verse 700, there is no reason to suppose that it contains three instances of thwarted stress. The accents do not necessarily have to fall on normally unstressed words or syllables, as the following scansion that Brooks and Warren might have suggested indicates:

/ / / U / U / U U / U
Right so | let it | be by | wrytynge | amendid

Again the pattern of stresses is the same if the line is read rhythmically:

/ / / U / U / U U / U
| ♪. | ♩ 𝄾 | ♪. ♪. | ♩ ♪ | ♪ ♪ ♪ | ♪ ♪
Right so / let it be by wrytynge amendid

[14] The musical notation is modeled after Southworth.

Similar remarks can be made about other metrical studies of Hoccleve which presuppose a rigidified iambic pattern. Some of the examples of thwarted stress pointed out by W. J. Courthope[15] (from the *Compleynte of the Virgin*) can easily be scanned as lines containing inversion and substitution:

/ / U U / U / U /
Thee | norissh|yng faire | & ten|drely
[v. 77]

U / U / / U U / U /
Þat al|le folk | see and | beholde | it may[16]
[v. 87]

U / / U /U U / U /
As thow | were an | euel | & wik|kid wight
[v. 92]

/U U / / U U / U /U
Sone, | if thow | haddist | a fad|ir lyuynge
[v. 102]

Other scansions and readings are possible which would also avoid the placing of verse accents on normally unstressed words or syllables. The last two lines, for example, can be read rhythmically as four-stress lines:[17]

U / U U /UU / U /
As thow were an euel & wikkid wight

/ U U / UU /U / U
Sone, if thow haddist a fadir lyuynge[18]

My point is that Hoccleve can be accused of thwarted stress only if one believes that he was supposed to write iambic decasyllables with an invariable pattern of verse accents.

A great many of the examples of "schwebende Betonung" given by Bock (see n. 3 above) can be more reasonably scanned as head-

[15] *A History of English Poetry*, I (London, 1895), 338-339.

[16] Hoccleve's autograph manuscript (Durham MS. Cosin V. III. 9) has *all* rather than *alle*. If Hoccleve did not intend that there be a syllabic final *-e*, the line would read less smoothly; but there would be no thwarted stress. The line would then resemble Lydgate's broken-backed line.

[17] I omit the musical notation. C. S. Lewis writes that very few of Hoccleve's lines will scan as "fifteenth-century heroics" (i.e., four-stress lines). "At this point no one will forget Hoccleve's own statement that he was the friend and pupil of Chaucer. Have we here a real proof of this discipleship and, with it, a proof that Chaucer was writing true decasyllables but that the tradition . . . was very soon lost?" — "The Fifteenth-Century Heroic Line," *Essays and Studies by Members of the English Association*, XXIV (1938), 37-38. Professor Southworth would answer No to the latter part of Lewis' question.

[18] Southworth would not pronounce the final *-e* in *Sone*.

less lines, broken-backed lines, lines containing one or more metrical inversions, or combinations of these. In the following list I have given first the scansion suggested by Bock, then a scansion which removes verse accents from weak words and syllables, and finally one or more readings of the line as a verse of cadence (omitting the musical notation).[19]

Regement of Princes, v. 460:

/
It is syn-ne outragious and vyl

/ U / U / U / U /
It | is synne | outra|gious | and vyl [Type D]

or

U U / U / U / U /
It is synne outragious and vyl

or

/ U / U / UU U /
It is synne outragious and vyl

or perhaps

U U / U / UU U /
It is synne outragious and vyl

Regement of Princes, v. 613:

/ / /
By þat sette I naght þe worþ of a flye

U / / U / U / U U /
By þat | sette | I naght | þe worþ | of a flye [C]

or

U / U U / U / U U /
By þat sette I naght þe worþ of a flye

Regement of Princes, v. 849:

/ / /
Of þis wreched worldes affeccioun

/ U / U / U U / U /
Of | þis wrech|ed world|es affec|cioun [D]

or

U U / U / U U / U /
Of þis wreched worldes affeccioun

[19] Each line that I have *scanned* could be *read* as a verse of cadence with the same pattern of stresses. But as verses of cadence the lines might also be read with different patterns of stresses (which I indicate). Southworth himself admits that he does not always read the same line in the same way (*Verses of Cadence,* p. 9).

Regement of Princes, v. 974:

/ / /
VI marc, yeerly, and no mor-e þan þat

/ ∪ / ∪ / ∪ / ∪ /
VI | marc, yeer|ly, and | no more | þan þat [D]

or

/ / / ∪ ∪ ∪ / ∪ /
VI marc, yeerly, and no more þan þat

Regement of Princes, v. 5091:

/ /
Whan þe gretter obeith to þe lesse

/ ∪ / ∪ ∪ / ∪ / ∪ /
Whan | þe gretter | obe|ith to | þe lesse [B plus D]

or

/ ∪ / ∪ ∪ / ∪ ∪ ∪ /
Whan þe gretter obeith to þe lesse

or

∪ ∪ / ∪ ∪ / ∪ / ∪ /
Whan þe gretter obeith to þe lesse

or perhaps

∪ ∪ / ∪ ∪ / ∪ ∪ ∪ /
Whan þe gretter obeith to þe lesse

Compleynte of the Virgin, v. 177:

/
As I to thee straung-e were and vnknowe

∪ / ∪ / / ∪ / ∪ ∪ /
As I | to thee | straung|e were | and vnknowe [C]

or

∪ / ∪ / / / ∪ ∪ /
As I to thee straunge were and vnknowe

Address to Sir John Oldcastle, v. 2:

/ /
Comandith vs if our brothir be falle

∪ / ∪ / / ∪ / ∪ ∪ /
Comand|ith vs | if | our broth|ir be falle [C]

or

∪ / ∪ / ∪ ∪ / ∪ ∪ /
Comandith vs / if our brothir be falle

Many of Licklider's examples of arsis-thesis variation can be scanned in a different fashion. In the following list I have given first the scansion suggested by Licklider (pp. 202 ff.), then a scansion which removes the arsis-thesis variation, and finally a reading of the line as a verse of cadence.[20]

Address to Sir John Oldcastle, v. 178:

U / / U
It is no manhode it is cowardyse

/ U U / U / U / U /
It is | no man|hode it | is cow|ardyse

or

U U / / U U U / U /
It is no manhode / it is cowardyse

Tale of Jereslaus' Wife, v. 325:

/ U U /
O wilt thow so wilt thow make it so strange

U / U / / U / U U /
O wilt | thow so | wilt | thow make | it so strange [C]

or

/ / U / / U / U U /
O / wilt thow so / wilt thow make it so strange

Lerne to Dye, v. 128:

/ U /
But help is noon help and confort been dede

U / U / / U / U U /
But help | is noon | help | and con|fort been dede [C]

(If the line is read as a verse of cadence, the pattern of stresses can be *only* the same as in my suggested scansion.)

Lerne to Dye, v. 421:

/ U U /
O, herkneth now herkneth now alle yee[21]

U / U / / U / U /
O, herk|neth now | herk|neth now | all yee [C]

or

/ / U / / U / U /
O, herkneth now / herkneth now all yee

[20] Again, each line that I have *scanned* could be *read* as a verse of cadence with the same pattern of stresses.

[21] Hoccleve's autograph MS has *all* rather than *alle* (see n. 16).

Dialogue with a Friend, v. 295:

∪ /
Yis, Thomas, yis thow hast a good entente

/ / ∪ / ∪ / ∪ / ∪ /
Yis, Thom|as, yis | thow hast | a good | entente

or

/ / ∪ / / ∪ ∪ / ∪ /
Yis, Thomas, yis / thow hast a good entente

The foregoing illustrations show that many lines by Hoccleve have no instances of thwarted stress unless one presupposes that the poet wrote iambic decasyllables with an invariable pattern of stresses. Many lines that have heretofore been pointed out as examples of arsis-thesis variation, thwarted stress, or simply bad meter can actually be scanned in a smooth way through recognition of metrical inversion and substitution and through an understanding of Schick's types. They can be *read* in a smooth way as verses of cadence. The often repeated dictum that Hoccleve had no metrical competence is untenable. What scholars have called his want of metrical skill is a value judgment that can be traced back to an absurd theory of English pentameter line structure. There is no thwarted stress in Hoccleve.

CHAPTER VI

HOCCLEVE AND CHAUCER

1. THE *REGEMENT* PORTRAITS OF CHAUCER

One of the best-known aspects of Hoccleve's career is something altogether extra-literary: he was responsible for perhaps the most authentic portrait of Chaucer that has come down to us. It appears in the *Regement of Princes,* Brit. Mus. MS. Harl. 4866, leaf 91. The manuscript is not in Hoccleve's handwriting, but it belongs to the first quarter of the fifteenth century. The portrait, half-length, has a background of green tapestry. Chaucer is obviously advanced in age. He is depicted with greyish white hair and a beard, which is biforked. He wears a dark-colored robe and hood. Suspended from a cord around his neck is a small black case, containing presumably a knife or pen. In his left hand he holds a string of beads, and with his right hand he points to this place in Hoccleve's text: "I haue heere his lyknesse / Do make . . ." (vv. 4995-96). Of all the descriptions of the portrait I have seen, Furnivall's is the most arresting. It is subjective, but unusually perceptive:

> The face is wise and tender, full of a sweet and kindly sadness at first sight, but with much bonhommie in it on a further look, and with deepset, farlooking, grey eyes. Not the face of a very old man, a totterer, but of one with work in him yet, looking kindly, though seriously, out on the world before him. Unluckily, the parted grey moustache, and the vermilion above and below the lips, render it difficult to catch the expression of the mouth; but the lips seem parted, as if to speak. . . . One feels one would like to go to such a man when one was in trouble, and hear his wise and gentle speech.[1]

Various types of reproductions can be found in many places. One closely resembling the manuscript is the full-sized photograph in black and white of leaf 91, portrait and text, that appears in the Chaucer Society edition of M. H. Spielmann's *Portraits of Geoffrey*

[1] *Trial-Forewords to My "Parallel-Text Edition of Chaucer's Minor Poems" for the Chaucer Society*, Chaucer Soc., 2nd Ser., No. 6 (London, 1871), p. 93.

Chaucer.[2] Hoccleve did not draw the portrait himself but rather had someone do it for him, as, in fact, the above-cited verse indicates.

The Harleian portrait is especially significant because most later portraits ultimately derive from it. Spielmann has shown that the portrait in Brit. Mus. MS. Addit. 5141, the two portraits in the Bodleian Library, and the Sloane, Fairfax Murray, and Clarendon portraits all owe a great deal to the work of the early fifteenth-century artist. Even the well-known equestrian drawing of Chaucer in the Ellesmere manuscript of the *Canterbury Tales* is probably based on the Hoccleve portrait. Brusendorff has observed that "the awkward disparity in size between the rider's body and his legs and horse, a lack of proportion not seen in the other figures, clearly shows that the horse was added later and that a half-length picture like that in Harl. 4866 in this way has been converted into the Ellesmere equestrian portrait."[3]

A second portrait of Chaucer can be found in another early fifteenth-century manuscript of the *Regement* — Brit. Mus. MS. Royal 17. D. vi, which Thomas Wright edited in 1860 for the Roxburghe Club. The portrait appears in the left-hand margin of the backside of leaf 90. Unlike the better-known Harleian portrait, it shows the figure of Chaucer in full length. Chaucer is looking toward the right-hand side of the page; he holds a string of beads in his right hand; and he is pointing with his left index finger to these lines: "That they that haue of hym · lost thought and mynde / By this peynture · may ageyn hym fynde" (from the MS; vv. 4997-98 in Furnivall's text). The Royal portrait has been reproduced very infrequently. There is a black-and-white photograph in Spielmann and a slightly touched-up replica in the *British Museum Catalogue of Western MSS in the Old Royal and King's Collections* (Vol. IV, pl. 101). The details of Chaucer's facial features are not so carefully executed as in the Harleian portrait, but the drawing is not without value. It is one of the earliest pictorial representations of Chaucer, and it is large and clear enough to complement our knowledge of Chaucer's physical appearance derived from other manuscript drawings and from his own words. Because of this portrait and also the

[2] 2nd Ser., No. 31 (London, 1900). The work was published originally in *Chaucer Memorial Lectures, 1900* (London, 1900), pp. 111-141. To my knowledge no photograph in color has ever been published.

[3] Aage Brusendorff, *The Chaucer Tradition* (London and Copenhagen, 1925), p. 17.

large illumination of Hoccleve offering his *Regement* to Prince Henry (which is reproduced in the present study as the frontispiece), Wright thought that the Royal MS was the very book Hoccleve gave to the prince. This is possible, but unlikely, since the book is not in Hoccleve's handwriting. Unlike the famous Harleian portrait, the Royal portrait has had no appreciable influence on later paintings and portraits of Chaucer.

There are forty-four fifteenth-century manuscripts of the *Regement of Princes,* some of them complete, others lacking varying numbers of stanzas, and three containing mere excerpts.[4] Brusendorff examined twenty-eight of the forty-four, discovering only two Chaucer portraits — in Harley 4866 and Royal 17. D. vi. Traces of the portrait are still visible in Harley 4826; but "sum ffuryous ffoole" cut out the portrait itself, and it is now lost.[5] The whole leaf containing the stanzas on Chaucer and presumably the portrait has been cut out of Arundel 38. But this manuscript still contains a fine portrait of Hoccleve, on his knees, presenting a copy of the *Regement* to Prince Hal.[6] In Camb. Un. Gg. 6. 17 Brusendorff observes that "the five stanzas praising Chaucer and describing his picture are entirely omitted, the loss occurring between the first and second stanzas on a page; probably the leaf containing them was cut out of the scribe's copy for the sake of the picture, or they may have been omitted because the corresponding portrait was wanting" (p. 15). The remaining manuscripts that Brusendorff examined, finding no portrait, are Bodl. 1504 (Laud 735), Bodl. 1786 (Digby 185), Bodl. 6920 (Ashmole 40), Bodl. 14503 (Rawl. Poet. 10), Bodl. 14660 (Rawl. Poet. 168), Bodl. 21732 (Douce 158), Camb. Un. Hh. 4. 11, Camb. Un. Kk. 1. 3, Trinity Camb. 602 (R. 3. 22), Fitz-

[4] See Carleton Brown and Rossell Hope Robbins, *The Index of Middle English Verse* (New York, 1943), p. 351.

[5] In the lower margin of the page appears this poem, written in a late sixteenth-century hand:

Off worthy Chawcers   Sum ffuryous ffoole
here the picture stood   have Cutt the Same in twayne
That much did wright   his deed doe shewe
and all to doe us good   he bore a barren Brayne

[Brusendorff's transcription, p. 14, n. 2]

[6] The best reproduction is in Richard Wülker's *Geschichte der Englischen Litteratur* . . . (Leipzig and Vienna, 1896), facing p. 169. Brusendorff refers *mistakenly* to additional portraits of Hoccleve in Harley 4826 and Camb. Un. Hh. 4. 11 (p. 15, n. 1). I have examined both MSS. The former contains a portrait of Lydgate and the latter no portrait at all.

william Mus. McClean 182, Fitzwilliam Mus. McClean 185, Arundel 59, Harley 116, Harley 372, Harley 7333, Royal 17. C. xiv, Royal 17. D. xviii, Royal 17. D. xix, Sloane 1212, Sloane 1825, BM Addit. 18632, Advocates 19. 1. 11, and Univ. of Edinb. 202 (D. b. vi. 7).[7]

Two manuscripts of the *Regement* not examined by Brusendorff that are now in the Huntington Library — HM 135 (*olim* Phillipps 8980) and EL 26. A. 13 (*olim* Ellesmere) — do not contain the Chaucer portrait. Nor does Garrett 137 (*olim* Ashburnham 244), now in the Princeton University Library. Nor do Bodl. 3441 (Selden supra 53), Bodl. 6533 (Dugdale 45), Bodl. 27627 (Bodley 221), Corp. Christi Camb. 496, Pepys 2101, Queens' Camb. 12, St. John's Camb. 223, Soc. of Antiquaries 134, and Merton 28.[8] Indeed, the only other manuscript still containing the portrait is Rosenbach 594 (*olim* Phillipps 1099), of the second half of the fifteenth century. Henry J. Todd refers to this portrait in his *Illustrations of the Lives and Writings of Gower and Chaucer,* describing it with the adjective "indifferent."[9] Skeat alludes to it very briefly in his Life of Chaucer prefixed to the first volume of *The Complete Works of Geoffrey Chaucer.*[10] K. Schümmer mentions it in his edition of Walton's *Consolation of Philosophy* and mistakenly gives the number of the Phillipps manuscript as 1022 instead of 1099.[11] Brusendorff repeats the mistake in *The Chaucer Tradition* (p. 14, n. 1). He was aware of the existence of this third portrait but had never actually examined the manuscript containing it nor seen a reproduction of it. Reginald Call notes its existence in his article on the Plimpton portrait of Chaucer.[12]

The Rosenbach portrait has never been published in any study of the portraits of Geoffrey Chaucer. It has scarcely been mentioned

[7] Brusendorff refers to "a MS. of Hoccleve's poem at Oxford, Balliol Coll. 329" (p. 15, n. 3). Again he is mistaken. The Balliol College MS contains, among other things, Lydgate and Burgh's poetical version of the *Secreta Secretorum* — not Hoccleve's *Regement.* See R. A. B. Mynors, *Catalogue of the Manuscripts of Balliol College Oxford* (Oxford, 1963), pp. 339-340.

[8] I have written to all the libraries containing manuscripts of the *Regement* not examined by Brusendorff. The various curators of manuscripts have kindly furnished me with information regarding the Chaucer portrait.

[9] (London, 1810), p. xxxi.

[10] 2nd ed. (Oxford, 1899), p. lx.

[11] Bonner Studien zur Englischen Philologie, VI (Bonn, 1914), p. xii.

[12] "The Plimpton Chaucer and Other Problems of Chaucerian Portraiture," *Speculum,* XXII (1947), 140, n. 42. Call does not know for certain how many manuscripts of the *Regement* contain the portrait.

in print and never discussed. I reproduce it here (following p. 116), since the only other reproduction available, that of the Rosenbach Company,[13] is not well known and cannot be found in most libraries. In no way does it deserve to be called "indifferent." It is unquestionably one of the clearest manuscript portraits of Chaucer that we have. But it adds really nothing to our knowledge of Chaucer's physical appearance because it is an almost exact replica of the portrait in Harl. MS. 4866. The illuminator apparently made his drawing either directly from the earlier Harleian portrait or from one just like it. Even the coloring is similar. The two main points of contrast are (1) that the diaper pattern in the background is much clearer in the Rosenbach portrait and (2) that the portrait is so positioned that Chaucer's right hand points to a place in the text ten lines above the place to which the hand in the Harleian portrait points. These differences of course have nothing to do with the actual figure of Chaucer. The differences that do relate to Chaucer are few. The folds in his garment in the Rosenbach portrait are brought out by black linear detailing on grey, whereas in the Harleian portrait we have just the opposite. In the Rosenbach portrait there is no wisp of hair above Chaucer's forehead. Other differences are too minute to warrant attention.

In summary, then, the only existing manuscripts of the *Regement of Princes* that contain the portrait of Chaucer are Harley 4866, Royal 17. D. vi, and Rosenbach 594; and the portrait in Rosenbach 594 is an almost exact replica of that in Harley 4866.

The miniature full-length portrait of Chaucer in Lansdowne MS. 851 does not resemble any of the Hoccleve portraits. Furnivall called it a "stupid peasant thing."[14] Of much greater significance is the well-known illumination of Chaucer reciting his *Troilus* before a courtly audience, from the manuscript of *Troilus and Criseyde* in Corpus Christi College, Cambridge (MS. 61). It has been reproduced in color to accompany Margaret Galway's article, "The 'Troilus' Frontispiece."[15] The manuscript was written in the first quarter of the fifteenth century, and it belonged at one time to Anne Nevil, daughter of Joan Beaufort (legitimized daughter of John of

[13] *An Exhibition of Fifteenth Century Manuscripts and Books in Honor of the Six Hundredth Anniversary of the Birth of Geoffrey Chaucer*, March 25 to April 30, 1940 (Philadelphia and New York, 1940), facing p. 16.

[14] Quoted by Spielmann, p. 11.

[15] *MLR*, XLIV (1949), 161-177.

Gaunt) and Ralph Nevil (Earl of Westmoreland). Brusendorff believes it is probable "that the countess of Westmoreland [i.e., Joan Beaufort] had the Corpus MS. transcribed from a family copy of Chaucer's *Troilus,* originally executed for her father John of Gaunt, probably in the 'eighties, and sumptuouosly decorated with pictures, of which the frontispiece showed the author reciting his poem at court" (p. 23). On the other hand it is possible, as Miss Galway indicates, that the extant miniature is the original portrait (p. 161). If this is so, the artist may have based his figure of Chaucer on a portrait like that in Harl. MS. 4866. Both are half-length portraits with the head, shoulders, and arms in approximately the same positions. If Brusendorff is right, however, it is then possible that the *Regement* portrait is derived from the *Troilus* frontispiece. And even if the extant miniature is the original, it possibly antedates the *Regement* portrait.

Hoccleve may have known the Countess of Westmoreland. He certainly thought of her as a patroness of literature, for he concluded his important "Series" group with an envoy to her. If there should have been a close connection between the poet and his noble patroness, is it possible that Hoccleve had access to the *Troilus* manuscript? Did he instruct his illuminator to model the *Regement* portrait after the *Troilus* portrait in its general contour — but to make Chaucer's facial features more aged, that is, as he himself remembered Chaucer at the turn of the century? These are questions that can probably never be answered. It is important, however, to observe that there is a striking resemblance between the two portraits with regard to the subject's posture and general appearance. The main difference is a question of age.

2. HOCCLEVE'S SUPPOSED FRIENDSHIP WITH CHAUCER

Hoccleve's verses on Chaucer, his "dere maistir," have often been admired by scholars and often included in anthologies. There are three separate passages, all to be found in the *Regement of Princes.*[16] In the first two Hoccleve praises Chaucer's ability as a poet and laments his death. In the third passage he is concerned primarily with the portrait of Chaucer, the drawing of which he personally supervised. On the basis of this material, which on the surface seems intensely personal, many writers have assumed that Hoccleve knew

[16] Furnivall's text, vv. 1958-74, 2077-2107, 4978-98.

Chaucer, studied under him, and saw him frequently during the 1390's. Furnivall writes that Hoccleve's reference to Chaucer's "bed mortel" (v. 1966) indicates in all probability that the pupil was present at the time of his master's death.[17]

An examination of this problem in a larger context shows that the personal relationship between the two poets is something that should not be pushed too far. Lines in praise of Chaucer occur often in fifteenth-century poetry. They can be found, to mention only a few examples, in the works of John Lydgate, John Walton, Osbern Bokenham, and George Ashby. Walton[18] praises Gower along with Chaucer, while Bokenham[19] and Ashby,[20] writing at a later time, include Lydgate also. No one has ever suggested that Walton and Bokenham were acquainted with Chaucer; and in the case of Ashby a personal relationship would have been impossible, since he was born at approximately the time of Chaucer's death. In the verse of these three writers the references to Chaucer are infrequent (perhaps occurring just once) and very brief. Lydgate's passages on Chaucer, in contrast, are both numerous and extended — even more so than those of Hoccleve.[21] Yet no one has ever argued that there was any kind of personal relationship between Chaucer and the Monk of Bury. In fact Lydgate expressly tells us, in discussing one of Chaucer's personal characteristics, that he had "herde telle" of it rather than knew about it at first hand.[22] Brusendorff suggests that whatever Lydgate knew about Chaucer's personal life he probably learned during the course of his contact with Chaucer's son Thomas.[23]

It has always been tempting to assume that there was a close personal relationship between Chaucer and Hoccleve because of the emotional element displayed in the latter's stanzas on Chaucer — something completely lacking in the above-mentioned passages from

[17] Hoccleve's *Minor Poems*, p. xxxi.

[18] *Consolation of Philosophy*, ed. Mark Science, E.E.T.S., O.S., No. 170 (London, 1927), st. iv — verses not numbered.

[19] *Legendys of Hooly Wummen*, ed. Mary S. Serjeantson, E.E.T.S., O.S., No. 206 (London, 1938 [for 1936]), vv. 1401-06.

[20] *Active Policy of a Prince*, vv. 1-7, included in *George Ashby's Poems*, ed. Mary Bateson, E.E.T.S., E.S., No. 76 (London, 1899).

[21] See Caroline F. E. Spurgeon, *Five Hundred Years of Chaucer Criticism and Allusion*, Pt. 1, Chaucer Soc., 2nd Ser., No. 48 (London, 1914 [for 1908]), pp. 14 ff.

[22] In the *Troy Book*, quoted by Spurgeon, p. 25.

[23] *The Chaucer Tradition*, pp. 31 ff.

¶ Mandatum est ut
diem sabbati sancti
fices.

Excellent prynce eek on the halidayes
Be war that ye nat youre conseyles holde
And for the tymes put hem in delayes
Thenketh weel this ye wel apayd be nolde
Yef youre soget nat be youre heste tolde
Right so oure lord god kyng and comaundour
Of kynges alle is wroth with that errour

In the long yer been werkedayes ynowe
Yf they be weel dispent so tentende
To conseyles to god youre herte bowe
Yf ye desyre men mygt hertis bende
To yow what kyng nat dredeth god offende
He nat rekketh do hym disobeysaunce
He shal be disobeyed eek parchaunce

¶ Commendacio
de Chaucer

The firste fyndere of oure fayr langage
Hath seyd in caas semblable and othir mo
So hyghly weel that it is my dotage
For texpresse or towche any of tho
Allas my fadir fro this world is go
My worthy maystir Chaucer hym I mene
Be thou advocat for hym heuenes queene

And thou wel knowist o blyssed virgyne
With lovyng hert and hy devocioun
In thyn honour he wroot ful many a lyne
O now thyn help and thy promocioun
To god thy sone make a mocioun
How he thy seruaunt was mayde marye
And lete his love floure and fructifye

Al thogh his lyf be queynt the resemblaunce
Of hym hath yn me so fressh lyflynesse
That to putte othir men in remembraunce
Of his persone I haue heere his liknesse
Do make to this ende in sothfastnesse
That they that han of hym lost thoght and mynde
By this peynture may ageyn hym fynde

Thymages that

Walton, Bokenham, Ashby, and even Lydgate. Brusendorff notes (p. 30, n. 3) that in all Lydgate's numerous allusions to Chaucer there is no "intimate personal cry" quite like this one from the *Regement:* "O maister, maister, god þi soule reste!" (v. 2107). Yet a close examination of Hoccleve's three passages on Chaucer reveals a singular lack of specific information about the supposed relationship between the two men. Hoccleve's allusion to Chaucer's "bed mortel" — something, as we have just noticed, that caught the attention of Furnivall — comes in an apostrophe to the deceased poet:

> Allas! þat þou thyn excellent prudence,
> In þi bed mortel mightist naght by-qwethe;
> What eiled deth? allas! whi wolde he sle the?
> [vv. 1965-67]

Of course the use of apostrophe (with or without rhetorical questions) is one of the most common features of early fifteenth-century poetic. I see no reason to assume that these lines imply an intimate relationship between Hoccleve and Chaucer, or indeed any personal relationship whatever. The following passage has also occasionally been pointed out as an indication of a close connection between the two poets:

> Mi dere maistir — god his soule quyte! —
> And fadir, Chaucer, fayn wolde han me taght;
> But I was dul, and lerned lite or naght.
> [vv. 2077-79]

Yet these lines tell us virtually nothing about the pupil-teacher relationship. Hoccleve may have tried to learn Chaucer's art by studying his works rather than studying under him in person. It is quite possible that this so-called autobiographical allusion is nothing more than a conventional expression of self-deprecation. The lines adjacent to the Chaucer portrait have also been cited as proof of the personal relationship between the two poets:

> Al-þogh his lyfe be queynt, þe resemblaunce
> Of him haþ in me so fressh lyflynesse . . .
> [vv. 4992-93]

But all that these lines really tell us is that Hoccleve had seen Chaucer while he was alive and still remembered how he looked. Hundreds of other people saw Chaucer too. Indeed it would have been unusual if Hoccleve had not seen Chaucer at one time or another, perhaps at Westminster. It does not follow, however, that there was any kind of personal relationship between the two men. Such a relationship would have been quite unusual. Geoffrey Chaucer, the friend of princes and favorite of royalty, and Thomas Hoccleve, an obscure clerk in the Privy Seal, moved in widely different social spheres.

The lack of specific information is all the more remarkable in view of other autobiographical passages in Hoccleve, which abound with specific, realistic details. If Hoccleve had really known Chaucer and studied under him, surely he would have had more to tell us. He might have described an especially memorable session which he had with his master; he might have written about Chaucer's physical appearance and his personal habits; and he might have given us specific information about Chaucer's dwelling at Westminster and his final illness. But the garrulous author of *La Male Regle,* the *Complaint,* and the *Dialogue with a Friend* tells us virtually nothing about his supposed encounters with Chaucer. Perhaps there never was a personal relationship between the two men. Neither Hoccleve's nor Chaucer's life records give indication of any such thing. If Hoccleve's passages on Chaucer seem heartfelt, perhaps all we should do is give him credit for developing, more convincingly than his contemporaries, what was essentially a poetic convention.

3. THE EXTENT OF HOCCLEVE'S INDEBTEDNESS TO CHAUCER

In reading through the voluminous works of Lydgate, one is constantly reminded of Chaucer. The Prologue to the *Siege of Thebes,* for example, opens with several long subordinate clauses introduced by the adverbial conjunction "when" — a construction obviously patterned after the opening lines of the General Prologue to the *Canterbury Tales.* During the course of Lydgate's Prologue there are frequent allusions to the Canterbury pilgrims, and unquestionably his portrayal of the Host owes much to Chaucer. Another example of his indebtedness to Chaucer is his description of spring in the second part of the *Testament.*[24] The passage is highly reminiscent of the opening lines of the *Canterbury Tales,* sometimes even in the choice of words:

Whiche sesoun prikkes fressh corages
[v. 297]

[24] Included in Lydgate's *Minor Poems,* ed. Henry Noble MacCracken, Pt. 1, E.E.T.S., E.S., No. 107 (London, 1911 [for 1910]), pp. 329-362.

First Zepherus with his blastes sote
Enspireth ver with newe buddes grene
[vv. 325-326]

In Hoccleve, allusions to Chaucer's poetry and echoes of his diction are not so frequent as one might expect. A few do occur, to be sure. In the *Letter of Cupid* Hoccleve's Cupid discusses Aeneas' mistreatment of Dido and then refers his readers to his "legende of martirs" (v. 316), in which they can find additional *exempla* of wronged ladies. The "legende of martirs" is probably to be equated with Chaucer's *Legend of Good Women.* "Chaucer speaks of the Legend of Good Women," Skeat explained, "as the 'Seintes Legende of Cupide,' or, as we should now say, Cupid's Legend of Saints [or Martyrs]."[25] Another allusion to a poem by Chaucer occurs in the *Dialogue with a Friend.* The Friend is speaking:

The wyf of Bathe, take I for auctrice
þat wommen han no ioie ne deyntee
þat men shoulde vp-on hem putte any vice;
I woot wel so / or lyk to þat, seith shee.
[vv. 694-697]

What he has in mind is apparently this passage from the Wife of Bath's Prologue:

I hate hym that my vices telleth me,
And so doo mo, God woot, of us than I.
[Robinson text, D 662-663]

Hoccleve's lines on the artistic conscience, also in the *Dialogue* (see end of Chapter IV), probably owe something to a more extended treatment of the same subject in the *Canterbury Tales* (A 725-746) — although it might be noted that similar passages occur in Jean de Meun and Boccaccio.[26] Still another passage reminiscent of Chaucer can be found in the *Dialogue:*

Thow woost wel / who shal an hous edifie,
Gooth nat ther-to withoute auisament,
If he be wys, for with his mental ye
ffirst is it seen / pourposid / cast & ment,
How it shal wroght been / elles al is shent.
Certes, for the deffaute of good forsighte,
Mis-tyden thynges / þat wel tyde mighte.
[vv. 638-644]

[25] Walter W. Skeat, "Hoccleve's 'Letter of Cupide,'" *The Academy,* XXXII (1887), 253.

[26] See Robert K. Root, "Chaucer and the Decameron," *Englische Studien,* XLIV (1912), 1-7.

The parallel material in Chaucer occurs in *Troilus and Criseyde:*

For everi wight that hath an hous to founde
Ne renneth naught the werk for to bygynne
With rakel hond, but he wol bide a stounde,
And sende his hertes line out fro withinne
Aldirfirst his purpos for to wynne.
[I.1065-69]

Both passages involve an analogy that comes ultimately from Geoffrey of Vinsauf's *Poetria Nova:*

Si quis habet fundare domum, non currit ad actum
Impetuosa manus: intrinseca linea cordis
Praemetitur opus, seriemque sub ordine certo
Interior praescribit homo, totamque figurat
Ante manus cordis quam corporis; et status ejus
Est prius archetypus quam sensilis.
[Faral text, vv. 43-48]

Hoccleve may have used Chaucer's stanza as a model; but in this case it is much more likely that he used the original Latin, or at least something other than the *Troilus* rendition, because he does not make Chaucer's mistake of translating *praemetitur* with the words "sende . . . out," as if the Latin had been *praemittitur* (or *praemittetur*).[27]

Several possible instances of Chaucer's influence on Hoccleve that were pointed out (but not discussed) by Furnivall[28] and Hammond[29] seem doubtful to me. In the Prologue to the *Regement of Princes,* Miss Hammond observed, the Beggar speaks of his wayward youth in language borrowed from Chaucer:

þere, þe former of euery creature
Dismembred y with oþes grete, & rente
Lyme for lyme, or þat I þennes wente.
[vv. 628-630]

Perhaps these lines owe something to similar passages in the Pardoner's Tale (C 472-476 and C 708-710). But there is no reason to believe that the quotation from the *Regement* is a clear instance of Hoccleve's use (conscious or unconscious) of Chaucer's language. Oaths that involved the dismembering of Christ's body were common in the Middle Ages. Many a person broke the third command-

[27] See F. N. Robinson's notes to his second edition of *The Works of Geoffrey Chaucer* (Boston, 1957), p. 818a.

[28] Hoccleve's *Minor Poems,* p. xl.

[29] Eleanor Prescott Hammond, *English Verse Between Chaucer and Surrey* (Durham, N.C., 1927), p. 56.

ment besides Hoccleve's Beggar and the three young revelers of the Pardoner's Tale. In fact, the use of oaths was a poetic convention in the popular tail-rhyme romances.

Furnivall claimed that "as the student reads Hoccleve, he will hear many echoes of Chaucer, and uses of his words and phrases." I would hesitate to state the matter as Furnivall did, because the implication is that Hoccleve borrowed from Chaucer. Moreover, Furnivall's short list of examples is singularly unimpressive. The words "waile and weepe" and "mortel fo" are surely not exhibitive of any borrowing on Hoccleve's part. And neither are expressions such as "to wax red for shame," "to be not worth a hawe," and "to jangle as a jay," which are clearly proverbial. If Furnivall's examples remind one of Chaucer, they perhaps do so merely because both poets were using the English language. They should not be considered clear-cut indications of Chaucer's influence on the younger poet. Even the *Tale of Jereslaus' Wife,* an analogue of the Man of Law's Tale, contains no noticeable traces of Chaucer's phraseology.

Despite the virtual absence of indisputable Chaucerian echoes in diction, the older poet's influence can sometimes be felt indirectly in other aspects of Hoccleve's poetic technique. Hoccleve's lively direct discourse in the Prologue to the *Regement of Princes,* in the *Dialogue with a Friend,* and in the two stories from the *Gesta Romanorum* may owe something to Chaucer. His occasional bits of humor are also vaguely reminiscent of Chaucer. Both these matters are connections between the two poets which a reader somehow senses but cannot prove with specific examples. In the more mechanical aspects of versification it seems too that Hoccleve owes something to Chaucer. With regard to stanzaic patterns he uses almost exclusively the rhyme-royal stanza, a form that Chaucer developed and then used extensively. Of course the use of this stanza became a tradition in the fifteenth century, much like the use of the heroic couplet in later times. The only other stanzaic pattern that Hoccleve uses to any appreciable extent is the eight-line pentameter stanza with a rhyme scheme of *ababbcbc,* this being Chaucer's Monk's Tale stanza. As far as rhyme is concerned, it has been shown that he follows Chaucer's usage in every respect except one: he sometimes rhymes *honoure* with words ending in *-ure.*[30] This

[30] Erich Vollmer, "Sprache und Reime des Londoners Hoccleve," *Anglia,* XXI (1899), 201-221.

one deviation on his part from Chaucer's practice is the main reason that has led scholars to ascribe the *Mother of God* to him rather than to Chaucer, who was once thought to be the author.[31] With regard to meter he follows Chaucer rather than Langland or the Pearl Poet; and yet his frequent use of headless and broken-backed lines places him closer to Lydgate than Chaucer.

These, then, are some of the intangible ways in which Chaucer's influence is perhaps felt in the work of Hoccleve. But the fact remains that there are very few direct allusions to Chaucer in Hoccleve's verse and almost no indisputable Chaucerian echoes in his diction and phraseology. Hoccleve's significance as a poet in his own right is obscured if he is categorized as a mere imitator of Chaucer. My discussion suggests that the amount of his indebtedness to Chaucer has been exaggerated.

. . . .

Throughout this book I have tried to arrive at a better understanding of Thomas Hoccleve by examining his works in the context of other fifteenth-century literature — something, I might add, that has never been done in a thoroughgoing way. I have also pointed out that some of the commonly held opinions about Hoccleve need reconsideration. The value judgments with regard to his meter, for example, are based on a theory of pentameter line structure that is not accepted by any recent student of Middle English verse. My examination of convention and individuality shows that the trappings of convention lie heavily on Hoccleve, who was very much a poet of his times; yet his verse contains many features that reveal a remarkable degree of individuality.

The autobiographical element is the most striking example of his individuality. A study of his themes and genres, on the other hand, reveals his indebtedness to his age. Yet in small ways he often managed to give his verse an individual stamp. In addition, he was a pioneer in introducing several well-known genres into English, such as the *Ars Moriendi,* the satirical panegyric of one's lady, and, especially, the manual of instruction for a prince. Hoccleve's poetic technique is best understood and appreciated in the context of other medieval literature. Like Lydgate and other fifteenth-century poets, he looked on poetry as versified rhetoric, he used word pairs fre-

[31] See Furnivall's edition of Hoccleve's *Minor Poems,* p. xxxix.

quently, and he treated his sources very freely. His originality as a craftsman consists mainly in his skillful handling of direct discourse. As for his relationship with Chaucer, the autobiographical significance of his often quoted lines in praise of Chaucer has been exaggerated. So also has the amount of his indebtedness to Chaucer in diction and phraseology.

Hoccleve's poetry can be read with enjoyment if one accepts the poetic of which he was an exponent and does not insist on looking for what is not there and was never intended to be there. In a sense my work is a plea for a better understanding of fifteenth-century poetic and a more liberal critical attitude toward some of the most readable literature of medieval England.

AN ANNOTATED HOCCLEVE BIBLIOGRAPHY

I BOOKS CONTAINING BIBLIOGRAPHICAL MATERIAL ON HOCCLEVE

I.1 Bale, John. *Scriptorvm Illustriũ maioris Brytannie, quam nunc Angliam & Scotiam uocant: Catalogus.* Basel, 1559. Page 537.

Describes Hoccleve's style with the words *lepidus* ("elegant") and *facundus* ("eloquent"). Remarks interestingly (but erroneously) that Hoccleve, according to the chronicler Thomas Walsingham (see item IV.69), followed the heretical doctrines of Wiclif and Berengarius. Goes on to say that Hoccleve, like Nicodemus, had to be a secret disciple of Christ because of his fear of the Papists. Concludes with a selective list of Hoccleve's works, including the "Series" group (i.e., the *Complaint,* the *Dialogue with a Friend,* the *Tale of Jereslaus' Wife, Lerne to Dye,* and the *Tale of Jonathas*) and the *Regement of Princes.*

I.2 Bennett, H. S. *Chaucer and the Fifteenth Century.* Oxford, 1947. Pages 285-286.

Useful, concise (but incomplete) bibliographical information.

I.3 Brown, Carleton, and Rossell Hope Robbins. *The Index of Middle English Verse.* New York, 1943.

Contains definitive lists of all manuscripts of Hoccleve's works. Notes that the *Regement of Princes* (of which there are 44 MSS) rates fifth among the longer Middle English poetical works preserved in the greatest number of manuscripts, the first four being the *Pricke of Conscience* (114 MSS), the *Canterbury Tales* (64 MSS), *Piers Plowman* (50 MSS), and the *Confessio Amantis* (49 MSS).

I.4 *The Cambridge Bibliography of English Literature,* ed. F. W. Bateson. Vol. I. New York, 1941. Pages 252-253. Vol. V (Supplement), ed. George Watson. Cambridge, 1957. Page 146.

Far from complete.

I.5 Hammond, Eleanor Prescott. *Chaucer: A Bibliographical Manual.* New York, 1908. Pages 434-436, 438-439, 444, 459-460.

Contains bibliographical information on poems by Hoccleve formerly attributed to Chaucer, namely, the *Letter of Cupid,* the *Two Balades to Henry V and the Knights of the Garter,* the *Legend of the Virgin and Her Sleeveless Garment,* and the *Mother of God.*

I.6 ———. *English Verse Between Chaucer and Surrey.* Durham, North Carolina, 1927. Pages 57-60.

A very useful (but incomplete) Hoccleve bibliography, including bibliographical material on Hoccleve manuscripts.

I.7 Mitchell, William Jerome. "Thomas Hoccleve: His Traditionalism and His Individuality: A Study in Fifteenth-Century English Poetic." Unpubl. diss. Duke, 1965. University Microfilms, Order No. 65-14,093.

The first chapter is an exhaustive survey of Hoccleve allusion, scholarship, and criticism. The dissertation concludes with a complete Hoccleve bibliography (slightly annotated).

I.8 Pits, John. *Relationvm Historicarvm de Rebus Anglicis.* Paris, 1619. Page 587.

Questions the notion that Hoccleve was a heretic. Concludes with a selective list of Hoccleve's works, adding nothing to Bale's list (I.1).

I.9 Ritson, Joseph. *Bibliographia Poetica: A Catalogue of Engleish Poets, of the Twelfth, Thirteenth, Fourteenth, Fifteenth, and Sixteenth, Centurys, with a Short Account of Their Works.* London, 1802. Pages 60-63.

Adds nothing to the Hoccleve canon which cannot already be found in Bale (I.1), Pits (I.8), Tanner (I.10), or Mason (II.A.1). Remarks that the Prologue to the *Regement of Princes* is "sufficiently prolix" and contributes to the confusion regarding the sources of the *Regement* by saying that it is "a free translation from the Latin of Aegidius de Columna" (cf. III.1). Believes that Mason selected for publication six pieces "of peculiar stupidity."

I.10 Tanner, Thomas. *Bibliotheca Britannico-Hibernica: sive, de Scriptoribus, qui in Anglia, Scotia, et Hibernia ad saeculi XVII initium floruerunt, literarum ordine juxta familiarum nomina dispositis Commentarius.* London, 1748. Page 557.

A much fuller entry than that of Bale (I.1) or Pits (I.8). Among the biographical details added are that Hoccleve worked for twenty years in the service of the keeper of the Privy Seal, that he had as a patron Humphrey, Duke of Gloucester, and that he studied law at Chester's Inn. (Tanner is probably wrong in this last detail. For at least part of Hoccleve's period of active duty the clerks of the Privy Seal were housed in Chester's Inn. Thus there is no need to assume that Hoccleve ever studied law.) Repeats the error that Hoccleve was a heretic but notes that he purged himself of all heresy in the Prologue to the *Regement of Princes.* States that the *Regement* is an English version of Egidio Colonna's *De Regimine Principum* (cf. III.1). Mentions *La Male Regle.* Includes among Hoccleve's works Lydgate's *Daunce Death* (i.e., *Dance Macabre*) and Chaucer's Knight's Tale. Gives valuable bibliographical information regarding Hoccleve manuscripts.

I.11 Tucker, Lena Lucile, and Allen Rogers Benham. *A Bibliography of Fifteenth Century Literature with Special Reference to the History*

of English Culture. University of Washington Publications in Language and Literature, Vol. II, No. 3. Seattle, 1928. Pages 223-225.
A useful (but incomplete) Hoccleve bibliography.

II EDITIONS

A General

II.A.1 Hoccleve, Thomas. *Poems by Thomas Hoccleve, Never Before Printed,* ed. George Mason. London, 1796.

The edition contains six poems from a manuscript then in Mason's possession (later Phillipps MS. 8151, and now Huntington Libr. MS. HM 111): (1) *La Male Regle,* (2) *Balade and Roundel to Mr. Henry Somer, Subtreasurer,* (3) *Balade, by the Court of Good Company, to Sir Henry Somer,* (4) *Balade to King Henry V for Money,* (5) *Balade to My Maister Carpenter,* and (6) *Balade to My Gracious Lord of York.* Mason comments on the autobiographical element in Hoccleve and suggests that his works show some degree of originality. Believes that in the *Tale of Jonathas* Hoccleve "indeed adheres closely to the substance of the story, yet embellishes it in various places by judicious insertions of his own" (p. 7). Objects to Warton's contention (IV.71) that the very titles of Hoccleve's poems "indicate a coldness of genius." Calls attention to Bale's error (I.1) in supposing that Hoccleve was a heretic.

II.A.2 ———. *The Minor Poems in the Phillipps MS. 8151 (Cheltenham) and the Durham MS. III. 9,* ed. Frederick J. Furnivall. *Hoccleve's Works.* Vol. I. E.E.T.S., E.S., No. 61. London, 1892.

The edition contains (A) all the poems in Phillipps MS. 8151 (now Huntington Libr. MS. HM 111), some of which had not been printed before: (1) *Compleynte of the Virgin Before the Cross,* (2) *Address to Sir John Oldcastle,* (3) *La Male Regle,* (4) *Balade to King Henry V on His Accession to the Throne,* (5, 6) *Two Balades to Henry V and the Knights of the Garter,* (7) *Ad Beatam Virginem,* (8) *Balade After King Richard II's Bones Were Brought to Westminster,* (9) *Balade to My Gracious Lord of York,* (10) *Mother of God,* (11) *Balade to the Duke of Bedford,* (12) *Balade to My Lord the Chancellor,* (13) *Balade and Roundel to Mr. Henry Somer, Subtreasurer,* (14) *Balade Put at the End of Hoccleve's "Regement of Princes,"* (15) *Balade to King Henry V for Money,* (16) *Balade to My Maister Carpenter,* (17) *Balade, by the Court of Good Company, to Sir Henry Somer,* and (18) *Balade to the Virgin and Christ;* (B) the *Letter of Cupid,* from Bodl. Libr. MS. Fairfax 16; and (C) the "Series" poems, from Durham MS. Cosin V. III. 9: (1) the *Complaint,* (2) the *Dialogue with a Friend,* (3) the *Tale of Jereslaus' Wife,* (4) *Lerne to Dye,* and (5) the *Tale of Jonathas.* Of special significance is Furnivall's "Appendix of Entries About Grants and Payments to Hoccleve, from the Privy-Council Proceedings, the Patent- and Issue-Rolls, and the Record Office" — information not known to earlier writers who had attempted biographical studies. Furnivall believes that Hoccleve's "chief merit" is "that he was the honourer and pupil of Chaucer" (p. xxv); that his meter is poor: "He constantly thwarts the natural run of his line by putting stress on a word that shouldn't bear it, or using a strong syllable as a weak one" (p. xli); that "the best parts of the Durham volume are Hoccleve's englishings of the two stories from the *Gesta Romanorum*" (p. xlv).

II.A.3 ———. *The Minor Poems in the Ashburnham MS. Addit. 133,* ed. Sir Israel Gollancz. *Hoccleve's Works.* Vol. II. E.E.T.S., E.S., No. 73. London, 1925 (for 1897).

The slender volume contains (1) *Inuocacio ad Patrem,* (2) *Ad Filium, Honor et Gloria,* (3) *Ad Spiritum Sanctum,* (4) *Ad Beatam Virginem,* (5) *Item de Beata Virgine,* (6) *Item de Beata Virgine,* (7) *Story of the Monk Who Clad the Virgin by Singing Ave Maria,* (8) *Letter of Cupid,* (9) *Balade to King Henry V,* and (10) *Three Roundels.* These are all Hoccleve's poems in Ashburnham MS. Addit. 133 (now Huntington Libr. MS. HM 744) except *Lerne to Dye,* which Furnivall (II.A.2) had already edited from Durham MS. Cosin V. III. 9.

II.A.4 ———. *The Regement of Princes, A.D. 1411-12, from the Harleian MS. 4866, and Fourteen of Hoccleve's Minor Poems from the Egerton MS. 615,* ed. Frederick J. Furnivall. *Hoccleve's Works.* Vol. III. E.E.T.S., E.S., No. 72. London, 1897.

The text of the *Regement* is based on Brit. Mus. MS. Harl. 4866 "because," Furnivall writes, "it has the best portrait of Chaucer, and fewer superfluous final *es* [i.e., *e's*] and some older readings, than Reg. 17 D vi, which Thomas Wright [II.B.13] edited for the Roxburghe Club in 1860" (p. xvii). An appendix includes fourteen shorter poems, which Furnivall believed were by Hoccleve, from Brit. Mus. MS. Egerton 615 (cf. III.11 and III.18). (Only one of these, *A Lamentation of the Green Tree Complaining of Losing Her Apple,* is unmistakably the work of Hoccleve.)

B Important Editions of Individual Poems

II.B.1 Hoccleve, Thomas. *Address to Sir John Oldcastle.* Included in *The Poems, etc., of Richard James, B.D. (1592-1638),* ed. Alexander B. Grosart. [London], 1880. Pages 135-188.

Copied by James from what is now Huntington Libr. MS. HM 111. The only printed edition of this transcript. An outspoken anti-Catholic, James considered Oldcastle a great Christian hero. His notes to the poem are lengthy, rambling, full of quotations, and concerned primarily with religious matters.

II.B.2 ———. "Ballad by Thomas Occleve Addressed to Sir John Oldcastle, A.D. 1415," ed. Lucy Toulmin Smith, *Anglia,* V (1882), 9-42.

From Phillipps MS. 8151 (now Huntington Libr. MS. HM 111). A careful edition with an introduction discussing (1) Sir John

Oldcastle's connection with the Lollard movement, (2) the life of Hoccleve, and (3) Richard James's interest in the poem (see II.B.1). The material on Hoccleve's life is based exclusively on the autobiographical poems then in print (i.e., *La Male Regle,* the Prologue to the *Regement,* and some of the short begging poems).

II.B.3 ———. *An Indigent Author* (i.e., *Balade to My Lord the Chancellor*). Included in *Secular Lyrics of the XIVth and XVth Centuries,* ed. Rossell Hope Robbins. Oxford, 1952. Pages 99-100.

From Huntington Libr. MS. HM 111.

II.B.4 ———. *A lamentacioun of the grene tree, complaynyng of the losyng of hire appill* (i.e., *Compleynte of the Virgin Before the Cross*). Included in *The book of the pylgremage of the sowle late translated out of Frensshe into Englysshe.* Westemestre: William Caxton, 1483. Folios lxiiij[v]-lxviii[v].

Printed along with thirteen other poems included in the English translation, made in 1413, of a French prose version of Guillaume de Deguileville's *Pèlerinage de l'Ame* (cf. II.A.4). No indication that the poem is by Hoccleve.

II.B.5 ———. *Letter of Cupid.* Included in *An English Garner: Ingatherings from Our History and Literature,* ed. Edward Arber, Vol. IV. Westminster, 1895. Pages 54-71.

From Urry's 1721 edition of Chaucer.

II.B.6 ———. *Letter of Cupid.* Included in *Chaucerian and Other Pieces,* ed. Walter W. Skeat. *The Complete Works of Geoffrey Chaucer.* Supplementary Volume. Oxford, 1897. Pages 217-232.

From Bodl. Libr. MS. Fairfax 16.

II.B.7 ———. *Letter of Cupid.* Included in *Fifteenth Century Prose and Verse,* ed. Alfred W. Pollard. Westminster, 1903. Pages 13-31.

The Urry text, revised with the aid of collations published by Skeat in *Chaucerian and Other Pieces* (II.B.6).

II.B.8 ———. *Letter of Cupid.* Included in *The Bannatyne Manuscript,* ed. W. Tod Ritchie, Vol. IV. Scottish Text Society, New Series, No. 26. Edinburgh and London, 1930. Pages 49-64.

II.B.9 ———. *The Monk and Our Lady's Sleeves* (i.e., *Legend of the Virgin and Her Sleeveless Garment*). Included in *The Middle English Miracles of the Virgin,* ed. Beverly Boyd. San Marino, California, 1964. Pages 50-53; notes, pp. 119-122.

From Huntington Libr. MS. HM 744, collated with Christ Church Oxf. MS. 152 and Trinity Col. Camb. MS. R. 3. 21. In the notes Miss Boyd comments on the background of the poem (see also III.6) and the relationship of the three manuscripts.

II.B.10 ———. *Mother of God.* Printed in a note entitled "Inedited Poem by Chaucer," *Notes and Queries,* First Series, XII (1855), 140-141.

From Advocates' Libr. Edinb. MS. 18. 2. 8, collated with the printing by John Leyden in 1801.

II.B.11 ———. *Mother of God.* Included in *A Parallel-Text Edition of Chaucer's Minor Poems,* ed. Frederick J. Furnivall. Chaucer Society, First Series, No. 57. London, 1879. Pages 137-144.

A parallel-text edition of the poem as it appears in Phillipps MS. 8151 (now Huntington Libr. MS. HM 111), Bodl. Libr. MS. Arch. Seld. B. 24, and Advocates' Libr. Edinb. MS. 18. 2. 8.

II.B.12 ———. *A New Ploughman's Tale: Thomas Hoccleve's Legend of the Virgin and Her Sleeveless Garment, with a Spurious Link,* ed. Arthur Beatty. Chaucer Society, Second Series, No. 34. London, 1902.

From Christ Church Oxf. MS. 152, paralleled with Gollancz's text (II.A.3). In this manuscript the poem appears with a spurious headlink as the Ploughman's Tale of Chaucer's *Canterbury Tales* (see I.5).

II.B.13 ———. *The Regement of Princes,* ed. Thomas Wright for the Roxburghe Club. London, 1860.

From Brit. Mus. MS. Royal 17. D. vi. The first printed edition. In the preface Wright comments on the autobiographical element in Hoccleve. He is interested in the *Regement* primarily as a social and political document and believes "it would have little interest for us but for the frequent allusions to the events and feelings of the age in which it was written" (p. xiii).

II.B.14 ———. *Richard II Interred in Westminster* (i.e., *Balade After King Richard II's Bones Were Brought to Westminster*). Included in *Historical Poems of the XIVth and XVth Centuries,* ed. Rossell Hope Robbins. New York, 1959. Pages 106-108.

From Huntington Libr. MS. HM 111.

II.B.15 ———. *Tale of Jonathas.* Modernized by William Browne of Tavistock and incorporated into The First Eglogue of *The Shepheards Pipe.* London, 1620. Pages not numbered.

From what is now Durham MS. Cosin V. III. 9. Browne's modernizations are mostly changes in orthography, and often these play havoc with Hoccleve's versification. Thus there is some truth in Francis Douce's remark that the reviser "mutilated" the poem (IV.19). Near the end of The First Eglogue Browne praises Hoccleve's ability in narrative poetry.

II.B.16 ———. "Three New Chansons of Hoccleve," ed. Israel Gollancz, *The Academy,* XLI (1892), 542.

From Ashburnham MS. Addit. 133 (now Huntington Libr. MS. HM 744). The first appearance in print of Hoccleve's *Three Roundels* (cf. II.A.3).

II.B.17 ———. *To the Kinges Most Noble Grace; and to the Lordes and Knightes of the Garter* (i.e., *Two Balades to Henry V and the Knights of the Garter*). Included in *Chaucerian and Other Pieces,* ed. Walter W. Skeat. *The Complete Works of Geoffrey Chaucer.* Supplementary Volume. Oxford, 1897. Pages 233-235.

From Phillipps MS. 8151 (now Huntington Libr. MS. HM 111).

C Some Anthologies and Other Works Containing Selections from Hoccleve

II.C.1 Arber, Edward, ed. *The Dunbar Anthology. 1401-1508 A.D.* London, 1901. Pages 80-83.

Includes the stanzas lamenting the death of Chaucer from the *Regement of Princes.* Furnivall's text.

II.C.2 Bennett, H. S. *England from Chaucer to Caxton.* London, 1928. Pages 32-33, 50-53, 138-143.

Includes (1) Hoccleve's *Humorous Praise of His Lady,* (2) the stanzas on dress from the Prologue to the *Regement of Princes,* and (3) selected autobiographical passages from *La Male Regle* and the Prologue to the *Regement.* Furnivall's and Gollancz's texts.

II.C.3 Coulton, G. G. *Social Life in Britain from the Conquest to the Reformation.* Cambridge, 1918. Pages 163-169.

Includes selected autobiographical passages from *La Male Regle* and the Prologue to the *Regement of Princes.* Furnivall's texts, with emendations by Coulton.

II.C.4 Furnivall, Frederick J., ed. *Queene Elizabethes Achademy. . . .* E.E.T.S., E.S., No. 8. London, 1869. Pages 105-108.

Includes several of the stanzas on dress from the Prologue to the *Regement of Princes.* From Bodl. Libr. MS. Laud 735.

II.C.5 Hammond, Eleanor Prescott. *English Verse Between Chaucer and Surrey.* Durham, North Carolina, 1927. Pages 53-76.

Includes (1) *La Male Regle,* (2) *Balade and Roundel to Mr. Henry Somer,* (3) *Balade to My Maister Carpenter* — all from Huntington Libr. MS. HM 111; (4) *Three Roundels,* from Huntington Libr. MS. HM 744; (5) an extract from the *Dialogue with a Friend,* from Bodl. Libr. MS. Selden supra 53; and (6) the stanzas lamenting the death of Chaucer from the *Regement of Princes,* from Brit. Mus. MS. Arundel 38.

II.C.6 Kaiser, Rolf, ed. *Medieval English: An Old English and Middle English Anthology.* Third Edition. Berlin, 1959. Pages 498-500.

Includes selected stanzas (1) on dress, (2) in praise of Chaucer, and (3) on Hoccleve's work as a scrivener from the *Regement of Princes.* Furnivall's text.

II.C.7 Loomis, Roger Sherman, and Rudolph Willard, eds. *Medieval English Verse and Prose in Modernized Versions.* New York, 1948. Pages 347-351.

Includes in prose translation (1) extracts from *La Male Regle,* (2) the stanzas on Badby's heresy from the *Regement of Princes,* and (3) the stanzas in praise of Chaucer, also from the *Regement.* Based on Furnivall's texts.

II.C.8 Manly, John Matthews, ed. *English Poetry: 1170-1892.* Boston, 1907. Pages 47-48.

Includes (1) the stanzas eulogizing Chaucer from the *Regement of Princes* and (2) five stanzas from the *Address to Sir John Oldcastle.* Furnivall's texts.

II.C.9 Morley, Henry, ed. *Shorter English Poems.* London, 1876. Pages 56-64.

Includes (1) *Balade and Roundel to Mr. Henry Somer* and (2) *La Male Regle.* Mason's texts (II.A.1) with modernized spelling. Morley omits stanzas xviii-xx of *La Male Regle,* probably because he felt that the content was too bawdy for the general reader. Includes a black-and-white reproduction of Hoccleve's well-known portrait of Chaucer, from Harl. MS. 4866 (see IV.63), and a black-and-white sketch of Hoccleve presenting a copy of the *Regement* to Prince Henry, based on an illumination in Royal MS. 17. D. vi (reproduced in the present study as the frontispiece). The latter should not be confused with the better-known portrait in Arundel MS. 38, reproduced in color by Shaw (IV.57) and later by Wülker (IV.72).

II.C.10 Neilson, W. A., and K. G. T. Webster, eds. *Chief British Poets of the Fourteenth and Fifteenth Centuries: Selected Poems.* Boston, 1916. Pages 199-207.

Includes (1) four excerpts from the *Regement of Princes:* (a) "Extravagance in Men's Dress," (b) "Badby's Heresy," (c) "Woman's Superiority," and (d) "Tributes to Chaucer and Gower"; (2) *Balade and Roundel to Mr. Henry Somer;* (3) *Balade to My Gracious Lord of York;* (4) the Prologue and first five stanzas of Hoccleve's *Complaint;* and (5) several stanzas from *La Male Regle.* Furnivall's texts, with somewhat modernized spelling and capitalization.

II.C.11 Skeat, Walter W., ed. *Specimens of English Literature from the "Ploughmans Crede" to the "Shepheardes Calendar": A.D. 1394-A.D. 1579.* Oxford, 1871. Pages 13-22.

Includes (1) the stanzas in praise of Chaucer from the *Regement of Princes* and (2) the Story of John of Canace, also from the *Regement.* From Brit. Mus. MS. Royal 17. D. vi.

II.C.12 Spurgeon, Caroline F. E. *Five Hundred Years of Chaucer Criticism and Allusion, 1357-1900.* Pt. 1. Chaucer Society, Second Series, No. 48. London, 1914 (for 1908). Pages 21-23.

Includes Hoccleve's stanzas lamenting the death of Chaucer from the *Regement of Princes.* Furnivall's text.

II.C.13 Ward, Thomas Humphry, ed. *The English Poets.* Vol. I. London, 1880. Pages 124-128.

Includes the stanzas lamenting the death of Chaucer from the *Regement of Princes.* Manuscript on which the text is based is not indicated. Thomas Arnold, author of the short critical introduction, finds the Prologue to the *Regement* "considerably more interesting than the work itself" (p. 124).

II.C.14 Wülcker, Richard Paul, ed. *Altenglisches Lesebuch: Zum Gebrauche bei Vorlesungen und zum Selbstunterricht.* Vol. II. Halle, 1879. Pages 47-56.

Includes (1) most of the stanzas on peace from the *Regement of Princes,* from Harl. MS. 116 and Royal MS. 17. D. vi, and (2) part of *La Male Regle* — Mason's text.

III SPECIAL STUDIES

III.1 Aster, Friedrich. *Das Verhältniss des altenglischen Gedichtes "De Regimine Principum" von Thomas Hoccleve zu seinen Quellen nebst einer Einleitung über Leben und Werke des Dichters.* Diss. Leipzig, 1888.

An important study of the *Regement.* Gives (from early printed editions) the passages that Hoccleve borrowed from his three main sources — the *Secreta Secretorum,* Egidio Colonna's *De Regimine Principum,* and Jacobus de Cessolis' *Liber de Ludo Scacchorum* — together with the corresponding rhyme-royal stanzas. Shows that Hoccleve used the *Liber de Ludo Scacchorum* to the greatest extent. The last chapter discusses other possible sources. Aster's study of Hoccleve's life and works has been superseded by later scholarship.

III.2 Bennett, H. S. "Thomas Hoccleve." Included in *Six Medieval Men and Women.* Cambridge, 1955. Reprinted by Atheneum: New York, 1962.

A pleasant biographical sketch. Intended for the general reader rather than the scholar.

III.3 ———. "Thomas Hoccleve's Death." Letters to the Editor, *Times Literary Supplement* (25 December 1953), p. 833.

Points to evidence in the *Calendar of Close Rolls,* 1435-41, page 136, showing that Hoccleve could not have been living after the summer of 1437.

III.4 Bentley, Elna-Jean Young. "The Formulary of Thomas Hoccleve." Unpubl. diss. Emory, 1965. University Microfilms, Order No. 65-11,503.

An edition of Brit. Mus. MS. Addit. 24062 with an introductory discussion of the office of the Privy Seal. The manuscript is a formulary that Hoccleve prepared in 1423-24 for the use of future clerks of the Privy Seal. The work is businesslike, the most personal touch being a note in which Hoccleve apologizes for having inadvertently left blank space on a folio. This note and two or three brief directives to the reader are in English. Everything else is in Latin or French. See *Dissertation Abstracts,* XXVI (October 1965), 2154b-55a.

III.5 Bock, Franz. *Metrische Studien zu Thomas Hoccleves Werken.* Diss. Munich, 1900.

Concludes that Hoccleve's verse, while generally possessing the correct number of syllables, is full of instances of "schwebende Betonung": that is, the verse accents often fall on words and syllables that are unstressed in ordinary speech.

III.6 Boyd, Beverly. "Hoccleve's Miracle of the Virgin," *University of Texas Studies in English,* XXXV (1956), 116-122.

Argues that the poem "belongs to a group of miracles which deal with a form of worship known in the Middle Ages as Our Lady's Psalter, and in modern times as the rosary." Describes the genre and compares Hoccleve's poem with two other legends of Our Lady's Psalter. Finds Hoccleve's work "charming and graceful." See also II.B.9.

III.7 Buchtenkirch, Eduard. *Der syntaktische Gebrauch des Infinitiv in Occleve's De Regimine Principum.* Diss. Jena, 1889.

A grammatical study of Hoccleve's handling of various infinitive constructions, with remarks on Hoccleve's usage as compared with Chaucer's.

III.8 Häcker, Alfons. *Stiluntersuchung zu T. Hoccleves poetischen Werken.* Diss. Marburg, 1914.

A collection of numerous stylistic and rhetorical devices illustrated by copious excerpts from Hoccleve.

III.9 Hulbert, J. R. "An Hoccleve Item," *MLN,* XXXVI (1921), 59.

Points out a hitherto unnoticed document relating to Hoccleve's life.

III.10 Kern, J. H. "Die Datierung von Hoccleve's Dialog," *Anglia,* XL (1916), 370-373.

Discusses the various problems in dating the *Dialogue with a Friend,* deciding on a period between the end of March (or beginning of April) and the end of August, 1422.

III.11 ———. "Een en ander over Thomas Hoccleve en zijn werken," *Verslagen en Mededeelingen der Koninklijke Akademie van Wetenschappen,* Reeks 5, I (1915), 336-390.

Is interested mainly in biographical matters and the dating of Hoccleve's works. Discusses also three of the supposedly autograph manuscripts — Phillipps MS. 8151 (now Huntington Libr. MS. HM 111), Ashburnham MS. Addit. 133 (now Huntington Libr. MS. HM 744), and Durham MS. Cosin V. III. 9 — and concludes, on the basis of the many errors, that they are *not* Hoccleve autographs (cf. III.24). Discusses finally the question of whether Hoccleve wrote the fourteen poems in Egerton MS. 615 (see II.A.4), concluding, as did MacCracken (III.18), that with the exception of the *Compleynte of the Virgin,* he did not.

III.12 ———. "Hoccleve's Verszeile," *Anglia,* XL (1916), 367-369.

Argues that Hoccleve's lines consist always of ten or eleven syllables. Points out that some of the examples of irregularity given by Bock (III.5) come from the Egerton poems (not by Hoccleve) and from editions based on manuscripts containing many scribal errors.

III.13 ———. "Zum Texte einiger Dichtungen Thomas Hoccleve's," *Anglia,* XXXIX (1916), 389-494.

Scrutinizes all Hoccleve's poems printed by Furnivall for editorial mistakes, misprints, and scribal errors. Depends solely on printed texts and printed variant readings. Compares texts when two editions exist (e.g., the *Regement of Princes*) and tries to decide which has the more "correct" readings. Not accepting Phillipps MS. 8151 (now Huntington Libr. MS. HM 111) and Durham MS. Cosin V. III. 9 as Hoccleve autographs, Kern tries to reconstruct texts that Hoccleve might have written, free from all errors. Bases his emendations mainly on preconceived notions about late Middle English meter and syntax.

III.14 Kurtz, Benjamin P. "The Prose of Occleve's *Lerne to Dye*," *MLN*, XXXIX (1924), 56-57.

Observes that Hoccleve follows the original Latin (the Ninth Lesson for All Hallows' Day) closely but adds "tautological words or phrases." Believes the last paragraph is Hoccleve's invention.

III.15 ———. "The Relation of Occleve's *Lerne to Dye* to Its Source," *PMLA*, XL (1925), 252-275.

Compares Hoccleve's poem in detail with its Latin source (see III.16). Gives mathematical tables showing exactly to what extent and where in the stanza Hoccleve follows his original closely, alters it, or departs completely from it, adding material of his own. On the whole Kurtz is not impressed with Hoccleve's workmanship. Believes Hoccleve amplifies the original (often with word pairs) simply to overcome the exigencies of the rhyme-royal stanza. Admits, however, that here and there his additions are "not without some force."

III.16 ———. "The Source of Occleve's *Lerne to Dye*," *MLN*, XXXVIII (1923), 337-340.

Points out that Hoccleve's poem is based on the second chapter of the second book of Heinrich Suso's *Horologium Sapientiae*.

III.17 MacCracken, Henry Noble. "Another Poem by Hoccleve?" *JEGP*, VIII (1909), 260-266.

Prints a short religious poem (from Cambridge Univ. Libr. MS. Kk. 1. 6) beginning with the words "Heyle! be glad! & Joye withouten ende" and suggests, solely on the basis of style, the possibility of including it in the Hoccleve canon.

III.18 ———. "Hoccleve and the Poems by Deguileville," *The Nation*, LXXXV (1907), 280-281.

Decides on the basis of rhyme that the poems in Egerton MS. 615 (except for the *Compleynte of the Virgin*) are *not* the work of Hoccleve. Cf. II.A.4.

III.19 Mitchell, Jerome. "The Autobiographical Element in Hoccleve," *MLQ*, XXVIII (1967), 269-284.

Re-examines Hoccleve's autobiographical passages in relation to the work of his contemporaries and immediate predecessors and suggests that they reveal a degree of individuality unparalleled in Middle English poetry. (See Chapter I of this study.)

III.20 ———. "Hoccleve's Supposed Friendship with Chaucer," *ELN*, IV (1966), 9-12.

Questions the commonly held notion that Hoccleve was the friend and pupil of Chaucer. (See Chapter VI, Section 2, of this study.)

III.21 ———. "Thomas Hoccleve: His Traditionalism and His Individuality: A Study in Fifteenth-Century English Poetic." Unpubl. diss. Duke, 1965. University Microfilms, Order No. 65-14,093.

The doctoral dissertation from which the present study evolves. Concludes that despite Hoccleve's indebtedness to tradition, his verse contains many features that reveal a remarkable degree of individuality. See *Dissertation Abstracts,* XXVI (January 1966), 3927b-28a.

III.22 Ross, Charles H. "Chaucer and 'The Mother of God,' " *MLN,* VI (1891), 385-389.

Argues in favor of Hoccleve's authorship of the *Mother of God.* Reviews previous scholarship on the question.

III.23 Sandison, Helen Estabrook. " 'En Mon Deduit a Moys de May': The Original of Hoccleve's 'Balade to the Virgin and Christ.' " Included in *Vassar Mediaeval Studies,* ed. Christabel Forsyth Fiske. New Haven, 1923. Pages 233-245.

Prints the Anglo-Norman poem together with the corresponding parts of Hoccleve's *Balade.* Observes that Hoccleve's workmanship is somewhat better than mediocre. Comments briefly on patron Robert Chichele, who requested the translation.

III.24 Schulz, H. C. "Thomas Hoccleve, Scribe," *Speculum,* XII (1937), 71-81.

An important article. Argues convincingly that Huntington Libr. MS. HM 111, Huntington Libr. MS. HM 744, Durham MS. Cosin V. III. 9, and Brit. Mus. MS. Addit. 24062 are indeed Hoccleve autographs (cf. III.11). Discusses the date of Hoccleve's death, suggesting with good reason ca. 1430 rather than the traditional date, ca. 1450.

III.25 Skeat, W[alter] W. "Hoccleve's 'Letter of Cupide,' " *The Academy,* XXXII (1887), 253.

Points out an allusion to Chaucer in the *Letter of Cupid.* Argues that Cupid's "legende of martirs" (v. 316) should be equated with the *Legend of Good Women.* "Chaucer speaks of the Legend of Good Women as the 'Seintes Legende of Cupide,' or, as we should now say, Cupid's Legend of Saints."

III.26 ———. "Hoccleve's Rhymes and Chaucer's Virelays," *The Athenaeum* (4 March 1893), p. 281.

Points out that several of Hoccleve's balades are true virelays.

III.27 ———. "A Poem by Hoccleve," *The Academy,* XXXIII (1888), 325, 361.

Argues, mostly on the basis of the verses on heresy, that Hoccleve wrote the *Two Balades to Henry V and the Knights of the Garter* so often included among Chaucer's works. Did not know until later that the point had already been established by Mason (II.A.1).

III.28 Vollmer, Erich. "Sprache und Reime des Londoners Hoccleve," *Anglia,* XXI (1899), 201-221.

A thorough study of rhyme in Hoccleve. Shows that he follows Chaucer's usage in every respect except one: he sometimes rhymes *honoure* with words ending in *-ure.*

III.29 Williams, W. H. "Occleve, 'De Regimine Principum,' 299, 621," *MLR,* IV (1908-09), 235-236.

Suggests corrections for two of Skeat's glosses to the extracts from the *Regement* included in his *Specimens of English Literature* (II.C.11).

IV MISCELLANEOUS

IV.1 Baugh, Albert C., ed. *A Literary History of England.* New York, 1948. Pages 298-299.

Baugh observes that Hoccleve "seldom rises to the level of poetry." Goes on to say, however, that "his complete frankness, his many personal revelations, and his frequent references to current events make his verse almost always interesting."

IV.2 Bennett, H. S. *Chaucer and the Fifteenth Century.* Oxford, 1947. Pages 146-150.

Stresses Hoccleve's importance to students of social history. Gives a reliable, unbiased evaluation of his poetry, considering it somewhat better than mediocre. Believes its chief value is its "reflection of the poet's own ideas and personality" — "the naive outpourings of his own hopes and fears . . . presented to us in all their crude immediacy."

IV.3 Born, Lester K., ed. & trans. *The Education of a Christian Prince,* by Desiderius Erasmus. Columbia University Records of Civilization, XXVII. New York, 1936. Pages 120-124.

Summarizes Hoccleve's *Regement.*

IV.4 Brandl, Alois. *Mittelenglische Literatur (1100-1500).* Included in *Grundriss der Germanischen Philologie,* ed. Hermann Paul, Vol. II, Pt. 1. Strassburg, 1893. Pages 688-689.

A short, general discussion of Hoccleve's life and works.

IV.5 Brink, Bernhard ten. *History of English Literature.* Vol. II, Pt. 1, trans. Wm. Clarke Robinson. New York, 1893. Pages 212-220.

Believes that Hoccleve "comes nearer to [Chaucer] than almost any of the poets of the fifteenth century." Calls attention to his individuality — "Occleve has his own style" — and observes that he treats the two *Gesta* stories "with tact," has "happy moments" in both occasional and lyrical poems, and is generally successful when writing from his own observation. Praises the *Mother of God* very highly. Believes, however, that the *Address to Sir John Oldcastle* is "an extremely long-winded poem" and that Hoccleve's works are often marred by too much didacticism.

IV.6 Brooke, Stopford. *English Literature.* New York, 1880. Pages 42-43.

Finds Hoccleve "nothing but a bad versifier." Believes that the *Regement of Princes* marks the decay of Middle English poetry. Cf. IV.7.

IV.7 ———. *English Literature.* New York, 1897. Page 73.

A revised version of the aforenamed work. Following ten Brink (IV.5) Brooke admits that Hoccleve "had a style of his own." Believes that "in his playful imitations of Chaucer's *Balades,* and in his devotional poetry, such as his *Moder of God,* he reached excellence; but his didactic and controversial aims finally overwhelmed his poetry."

IV.8 Browning, Elizabeth Barrett. *The Book of the Poets.* Included in *Life, Letters and Essays of Elizabeth Barrett Browning,* Vol. II. New York, 1877. Page 22.

Rates Lydgate above Hoccleve but observes that neither was heir to Chaucer's artistry.

IV.9 Brusendorff, Aage. *The Chaucer Tradition.* London and Copenhagen, 1925. Pages 13-18.

Contains information on Hoccleve's portraits of Chaucer.

IV.10 *The Cambridge History of English Literature,* ed. Sir A. W. Ward and A. R. Waller. Vol. II. Chap. VIII, "The English Chaucerians," by George Saintsbury. Cambridge, 1930. Pages 204-208.

Criticizes Hoccleve's meter adversely (see also IV.52) but remarks that *Lerne to Dye* is "a really fine *Ars Sciendi Mori,* the most dignified, and the most poetical, thing Occleve has left us." Finds the autobiographical poems not unreadable. Believes that in narrative poetry "one merit Occleve may claim—that he has some idea how to tell a story."

IV.11 Campbell, P. G. C. "Christine de Pisan en Angleterre," *Revue de Littérature Comparée,* V (1925), 659-670.

Comments very briefly, page 662, on Hoccleve's rendition of Christine's *Epistre au Dieu d'Amours.*

IV.12 *Caxton's Book of Curtesye,* ed. Frederick J. Furnivall. E.E.T.S., E.S., No. 3. London, 1868. Stanzas li-lii.

Remarks that Hoccleve's language is "goodly," his *sententiae* "passing wyse," and his style of writing "playne."

IV.13 *Chambers's Cyclopaedia of English Literature,* ed. David Patrick, rev. J. Liddell Geddie. Vol. I. Philadelphia and New York, 1938. Pages 77-79.

A general discussion. Contains a fascimile reproduction in black and white of Hoccleve presenting a copy of the *Regement* to Prince Henry (from Brit. Mus. MS. Arundel 38).

IV.14 Coulton, G. G. *Medieval Panorama: The English Scene from Conquest to Reformation.* Cambridge, 1938. See Index for references to Hoccleve.

IV.15 Courthope, W. J. *A History of English Poetry.* Vol. I. London, 1895. Pages 333-340.

Emphasizes the autobiographical element. Finds the "Series" poems "not altogether wanting in a vein of original invention" and comments favorably on Hoccleve's use of dialogue. Criticizes his meter adversely, estimating that in 10 per cent of his lines the accents fall on weak syllables. Believes that grammatical inversion in Hoccleve (and Lydgate) is an unconscious return to Old English word order.

IV.16 Craik, George L. *A Compendious History of English Literature, and of the English Language, from the Norman Conquest.* Vol. I. New York, 1866. Page 402.

Does not rate Hoccleve highly. Believes his "endowment of poetical power and feeling was very small."

IV.17 *The Dictionary of National Biography,* ed. Sir Leslie Stephen and Sir Sidney Lee. Vol. IX. Article on Thomas Hoccleve by Frederick J. Furnivall. Oxford, 1921-22. Pages 950-951.

A good, short article by Hoccleve's chief editor.

IV.18 D'Israeli, I[saac]. *Amenities of Literature, Consisting of Sketches and Characters of English Literature.* Second Edition. Vol. I. New York, 1841. Pages 211-215.

Implies mistakenly that Hoccleve satirizes women in the *Letter of Cupid.* Finds his poetry "sufficiently uncouth," partly because "the language had not at this period acquired even a syntax."

IV.19 Douce, Francis. *A Dissertation on the Gesta Romanorum.* Included in *Illustrations of Shakespeare, and of Ancient Manners,* Vol. II. London, 1807. Page 390.

Observes that the Anglo-Latin *Gesta Romanorum* (rather than the continental *Gesta*) was Hoccleve's source and that modernizer Browne (II.B.15) "mutilated" the *Tale of Jonathas.*

IV.20 Ferguson, Arthur B. *The Indian Summer of English Chivalry: Studies in the Decline and Transformation of Chivalric Idealism.* Durham, North Carolina, 1960. Pages 176-177.

Comments on Hoccleve's attitude toward war.

IV.21 Fisher, John H. *John Gower: Moral Philosopher and Friend of Chaucer.* New York, 1964. Pages 62, 339.

Points out a hitherto unnoticed document relating to Hoccleve's life.

IV.22 Furnivall, Frederick J. *Trial-Forewords to My "Parallel-Text Edition of Chaucer's Minor Poems" for the Chaucer Society.* Chaucer Society, Second Series, No. 6. London, 1871. Pages 93-94.

Comments on Hoccleve's portrait of Chaucer in Harl. MS. 4866.

IV.23 Garnett, Richard. *English Literature: An Illustrated Record.* Vol. I. New York, 1903. Pages 192-194.

Rates Hoccleve below Lydgate in poetic merit but comments favorably on his lines in praise of Chaucer. Says that Hoccleve's references to Chaucer "are much more numerous than Lydgate's, reveal a much closer personal intimacy, and are marked by deeper feeling." (Actually, Lydgate's references to Chaucer are much more numerous than Hoccleve's.)

IV.24 Gilbert, Allan H. "Notes on the Influence of the *Secretum Secretorum," Speculum,* III (1928), 84-98.

Discusses Hoccleve's use of the *Secretum,* pages 93-98. Points out a few parallels between the *Regement of Princes* and the *Secretum* overlooked by Aster (III.1).

IV.25 Gray, Thomas. "Some Remarks on the Poems of John Lydgate." Included in *The Works of Thomas Gray in Prose and Verse,* ed. Edmund Gosse, Vol. I. London, 1902. Page 397.

Remarks that Lydgate's "choice of expression, and the smoothness of his verse, far surpass both Gower and Occleve."

IV.26 Grierson, Herbert J. C., and J. C. Smith. *A Critical History of English Poetry.* New York, 1946. Pages 44-45, 101.

The authors call the *Regement* "a hotch-potch of political wisdom" and the *Tale of Jonathas* "a silly tale."

IV.27 Hallam, Henry. *Introduction to the Literature of Europe in the Fifteenth, Sixteenth, and Seventeenth Centuries.* Second Edition. Vol. I. London, 1843. Page 122.

Observes that Hoccleve's poetry "is wretchedly bad, abounding with pedantry, and destitute of all grace or spirit."

IV.28 Hammond, Eleanor Prescott. *English Verse Between Chaucer and Surrey.* Durham, North Carolina, 1927. Pages 53-56.

A significant appraisal of Hoccleve's poetry. Comments on the autobiographical element, the stanzas lamenting the death of Chaucer, and the Harleian portrait of Chaucer (see IV.63). Praises Hoccleve's use of dialogue but comments unfavorably on his meter. Compares Hoccleve with Lydgate, observing that Hoccleve "is always livelier and simpler than Lydgate" and concluding that his verse is much less conventional than Lydgate's.

IV.29 Hecht, Hans, and Levin L. Schücking. *Die Englische Literatur im Mittelalter.* Wildpark-Potsdam, 1927. Pages 144-146.

Emphasizes the autobiographical element. Assumes that Hoccleve knew Chaucer personally and studied under him.

IV.30 Imbert-Terry, H. M. "The Poetical Contemporaries of Chaucer." Included in *Chaucer Memorial Lectures, 1900.* London, 1900. Pages 32-36.

Comments superficially on Hoccleve.

IV.31 Jacob, E. F. *The Fifteenth Century, 1399-1485.* The Oxford History of England, Vol. VI. Oxford, 1961. Pages 658-660.

Is interested in Hoccleve's work because of its reflection of social and political problems.

IV.32 James, Richard. *Iter Lancastrense; A Poem, Written A.D. 1636,* ed. Thomas Corser. Chetham Society, Vol. VII. Manchester, 1845. Pages lix-lx.

Refers to James's interest in Hoccleve's *Address to Sir John Oldcastle.*

IV.33 Jusserand, J. J. *A Literary History of the English People from the Origins to the Renaissance.* London, 1895. Pages 501-503.

Comments on the autobiographical element in Hoccleve's poetry and on the interest it holds for the historian. Believes his famous portrait of Chaucer (see IV.63) is "the best of his works."

IV.34 Kaluza, Max. *Englische Metrik in historischer Entwicklung.* Berlin, 1909. Pages 251-252.

Observes that Hoccleve, unlike Chaucer, sometimes stresses words and syllables that normally receive no stress.

IV.35 Kern, J. H. "Der Schreiber Offorde," *Anglia,* XL (1916), 374.

Discusses one of Hoccleve's colleagues in the Privy Seal.

IV.36 Kingsford, Charles Lethbridge. *English Historical Literature in the Fifteenth Century.* Oxford, 1913. Pages 230-231.

Is interested in the poems by Hoccleve that reflect the political and social milieu of the early fifteenth century. Concentrates on the Prologue to the *Regement of Princes.*

IV.37 Koch, J[ohn]. A Discussion of M. H. Spielmann's *Portraits of Geoffrey Chaucer* (see IV.63), *Englische Studien,* XXX (1902), 445-450.

Discusses Hoccleve's portraits of Chaucer in Harl. MS. 4866 and Royal MS. 17. D. vi.

IV.38 Legouis, Émile. *Le Moyen Age et la Renaissance.* Pt. 1 of Legouis and Louis Cazamian's *Histoire de la Littérature Anglaise.* Paris, 1924. Pages 153-154.

A very brief discussion of Hoccleve. Observes that the *Regement of Princes* is "clair, coulant, en vers encore assez corrects, mais la faiblesse intellectuelle et artistique du poème fait plus penser au didactique Gower qu'à Chaucer."

IV.39 Lewis, C. S. "The Fifteenth-Century Heroic Line," *Essays and Studies by Members of the English Association,* XXIV (1938), 28-41.

Observes, pages 37-38, that very few of Hoccleve's lines will scan as "fifteenth-century heroics" (i.e., four-stress lines).

IV.40 Licklider, Albert H. *Chapters on the Metric of the Chaucerian Tradition.* Baltimore, 1910. Pages 202-212.

Discusses "arsis-thesis variation" in Hoccleve.

IV.41 Lounsbury, Thomas R. *Studies in Chaucer: His Life and Writings.* Vol. III. New York, 1892. Pages 23-25.

Finds Hoccleve's tributes to Chaucer the only parts of his writings that deserve much attention. Believes that Hoccleve is overly sincere, especially in his self-deprecation, that in general he can be read only by someone with "dogged resolution," and that his *Letter of Cupid* is "tedious beyond description." Goes on to say, however, that "one or two" of the poems published by Mason (II.A.1) "have a distinct intellectual quality of their own." Praises the *Mother of God* highly, although uncertain it is the work of Hoccleve.

IV.42 Mendenhall, John Cooper. *Aureate Terms: A Study in the Literary Diction of the Fifteenth Century.* Lancaster, Pennsylvania, 1919. Pages 59-60.

Comments briefly on aureate diction in Hoccleve.

IV.43 Morley, Henry. *English Writers: An Attempt Towards a History of English Literature.* Vol. VI. London, 1890. Pages 122-134.

Emphasizes the autobiographical element.

IV.44 *The Muses Library; or, A Series of English Poetry,* ed. E[lizabeth] Cooper. London, 1741. Page 31.

Contains a brief biographical note on Hoccleve with a few lines from the *Regement.*

IV.45 Myers, A. R. *England in the Late Middle Ages.* Harmondsworth, Middlesex, 1952. Pages 166-167.

Reads Hoccleve's poetry for its reflection of social and political problems.

IV.46 Nicholas, Sir Harris. "Life of Chaucer." Included in *The Poetical Works of Geoffrey Chaucer,* ed. Richard Morris, Vol. I. London, 1891. Pages 83-84.

Discusses Hoccleve's portrait of Chaucer in Harl. MS. 4866.

IV.47 Pearsall, Derek. "The English Chaucerians." Included in *Chaucer and Chaucerians: Critical Studies in Middle English Literature,* ed. D. S. Brewer. London and Edinburgh, 1966. Pages 222-225.

A short, general discussion. Points out little that is new, but makes the interesting observation that Chaucerian echoes are not so frequent in Hoccleve as in Lydgate.

IV.48 Phillips, Edward. *Theatrum Poetarum, or A Compleat Collection of the Poets, Especially the Most Eminent of All Ages.* London, 1675. Part II, Supplement, p. 233.

A very brief discussion. Remarks that Hoccleve is famous for "being remember'd to have been the Disciple of the most fam'd *Chaucer.*"

IV.49 ———. *Theatrum Poetarum Anglicanorum: Containing the Names and Characters of All the English Poets, from the Reign of Henry III. to the Close of the Reign of Queen Elizabeth.* First Published in 1675, and Now Enlarged by Additions to Every Article from Subsequent Biographers and Critics. Canterbury, 1800. Pages 19-20.

Phillips' original entry on Hoccleve is expanded with selected passages from Warton's *History* (IV.71).

IV.50 Renwick, W. L., and Harold Orton. *The Beginnings of English Literature to Skelton, 1509.* New York, 1940. Pages 283-284.

The authors find the *Complaint* dull but remark that the *Gesta Romanorum* poems "are pleasant in their dilatory fashion" and that the *Regement* "may be dipped into for glimpses of a fifteenth-century life as well as a fifteenth-century mind." They commit the curious blunder of giving Hoccleve's surname as *John* rather than *Thomas.*

IV.51 Robbins, Rossell Hope. "Two Middle English Satiric Love Epistles," *MLR,* XXXVII (1942), 415-421.

Discusses Hoccleve's *Humorous Praise of His Lady* and other satirical panegyrics of one's lady.

IV.52 Saintsbury, George. *A History of English Prosody from the Twelfth Century to the Present Day.* Vol. I. London, 1906. Pages 231-234.

Criticizes Hoccleve severely for placing verse accents on syllables normally unstressed and not accenting syllables that should be stressed. States that the verse of both Hoccleve and Lydgate is "prosaic, hobbling, broken-backed doggerel."

IV.53 Sampson, George. *The Concise Cambridge History of English Literature.* Cambridge, 1941. Page 85.

Finds the autobiographical passages attractive.

IV.54 Schipper, J[akob]. *Englische Metrik.* Vol. I. Bonn, 1881. Pages 488-492.

Calls attention to Hoccleve's frequent placing of verse accents on words and syllables normally unstressed and his failure to accent words and syllables that should receive stress.

IV.55 Schirmer, Walter F. *Geschichte der Englischen und Amerikanischen Literatur von den Anfängen bis zur Gegenwart.* Second Edition. Vol. I. Tübingen, 1954. Pages 172-173.

Suggests the possibility that Hoccleve is not what he seems; that he assumes an overly righteous attitude in the *Address to Sir John Oldcastle* and sounds a highly patriotic note in the *Regement* because, in reality, he does not fully believe what he is writing and is afraid that others might suspect that he does not. Emphasizes the skeptical streak in Hoccleve, best illustrated by his *Humorous Praise of His Lady,* which looks forward to Skelton.

IV.56 Schlauch, Margaret. *English Medieval Literature and Its Social Foundations.* Warsaw, 1956. Page 293.

A very short discussion. Emphasizes the autobiographical element in Hoccleve's work and the reflection in it of early fifteenth-century London life. Refers mistakenly to the *Regement* as a translation of Egidio Colonna's *De Regimine Principum* (cf. III.1).

IV.57 Shaw, Henry. *Dresses and Decorations of the Middle Ages.* Vol. II. London, 1858. Pages not numbered.

Contains a reproduction in color of Hoccleve presenting a copy of the *Regement* to Prince Henry (from Arundel MS. 38).

IV.58 Skeat, Walter W. "Life of Geoffrey Chaucer." Included in his second edition of *The Complete Works of Geoffrey Chaucer,* Vol. I. Oxford, 1899. Pages lvii-lx.

Contains information on Hoccleve's stanzas in praise of Chaucer and on the Harleian portrait, which is reproduced as the frontispiece. Skeat's text of Hoccleve's stanzas on Chaucer is based on a collation of Wright's and Furnivall's editions of the *Regement of Princes.*

IV.59 Smith, G. Gregory. *The Transition Period.* Edinburgh and London, 1900. Pages 16-21.

Rates Hoccleve below Lydgate in poetic merit and remarks that his meter "is marred by wanton accentuation." Believes that the so-called personal element in Hoccleve (and Lydgate) is "more conventional and rhetorical, and of a pattern, than individual."

IV.60 Southworth, James G. *The Prosody of Chaucer and His Followers: Supplementary Chapters to "Verses of Cadence."* Oxford, 1962. Pages 72-76.

Elaborates on the earlier discussion in *Verses of Cadence* (IV.61).

IV.61 ———. *Verses of Cadence: An Introduction to the Prosody of Chaucer and His Followers.* Oxford, 1954. Pages 71-78.

Finds that Hoccleve's lines read well "rhythmically," as verses of cadence.

IV.62 Speght, Thomas. "Life of Geffrey Chaucer." Prefixed to his edition of *The Workes of our Antient and Learned English Poet, Geffrey Chavcer, newly Printed.* London, 1598. Pages of "Life" not numbered.

Remarks that the *Letter of Cupid* (which he prints, foll. 326^{v}-329^{r}) is by Hoccleve rather than Chaucer. Quotes Hoccleve's stanzas in praise of Chaucer and comments on them.

IV.63 Spielmann, M. H. *The Portraits of Geoffrey Chaucer.* Included in *Chaucer Memorial Lectures, 1900.* London, 1900. Reprinted separately (with corrections and larger plates) for the Chaucer Society, Second Series, No. 31. London, 1900.

Discusses and reproduces the Hoccleve portraits of Chaucer in Harl. MS. 4866 and Royal MS. 17. D. vi.

IV.64 Stowe, Iohn. *A Summarye of the Chronicles of Englande, from the first comminge of Brute into this Lande, vnto this present yeare 1570.* London, 1570. Foll. 252^{r}-252^{v}.

Quotes two stanzas on dress from the Prologue to the *Regement of Princes.*

IV.65 Tilgner, Elfriede. *Die Aureate Terms als Stilelement bei Lydgate.* Germanische Studien, CLXXXII. Berlin, 1936. Pages 77-78.

Does not find much aureate diction in Hoccleve.

IV.66 Tout, T. F. *Chapters in the Administrative History of Mediaeval England.* Vol. V. Manchester, 1930. Pages 54-112.

Discusses the office, household, and staff of the Privy Seal with many references to Hoccleve.

IV.67 Turner, Sharon. *The History of England During the Middle Ages.* Second Edition. Vol. V. London, 1825. Pages 335-340.

Believes that Hoccleve "has not had his just share of reputation." Emphasizes the autobiographical element and finds the *Gesta Romanorum* poems "not unworthy of notice." Believes that the poems printed by Mason (II.A.1) are Hoccleve's "least interesting productions."

IV.68 Utley, Francis Lee. *The Crooked Rib: An Analytical Index to the Argument About Women in English and Scots Literature to the End of the Year 1568.* Columbus, Ohio, 1944.

Lists and briefly discusses several poems by Hoccleve; see especially pages 110-111.

IV.69 Walsingham, Thomas. *Historia Anglicana,* ed. Henry Thomas Riley. Vol. I. London, 1863. Page 450.

Remarks that Wiclif followed the "damnatas opiniones Berengarii et Oklefe." (The "et Oklefe" is probably an erroneous scribal interpolation.)

IV.70 Warton, Thomas. *A Dissertation on the Gesta Romanorum.* Included in *The History of English Poetry from the Close of the Eleventh to the Commencement of the Eighteenth Century,* Vol. III. London, 1781. Pages lvi-lvii.

Refers briefly to Hoccleve's *Tale of Jonathas.*

IV.71 ———. *The History of English Poetry from the Close of the Eleventh to the Commencement of the Eighteenth Century.* Vol. II. London, 1778. Pages 38-44.

Remarks that Hoccleve "is a feeble writer, considered as a poet," and that the very titles of his poems "indicate a coldness of genius." Does not believe that the *Tale of Jonathas* deserves the praise bestowed on it by Browne (II.B.15). Admires Hoccleve's lines lamenting the death of Chaucer.

IV.72 Wülker, Richard. *Geschichte der Englischen Litteratur von den ältesten Zeiten bis zur Gegenwart.* Leipzig and Vienna, 1896. Pages 169-172.

Rates Hoccleve above Lydgate, commenting in particular on his originality, sense of humor, and lines in praise of Chaucer. Contains an excellent reproduction in color of Hoccleve presenting a copy of the *Regement* to Prince Henry (from Arundel MS. 38).

IV.73 Wylie, James Hamilton. *History of England Under Henry the Fourth.* 4 vols. London, 1884-98. See Index for references to Hoccleve.

IV.74 ———. *The Reign of Henry the Fifth.* Vol. I. Cambridge, 1914. See Index for references to Hoccleve.

IV.75 Zesmer, David M. *Guide to English Literature from Beowulf Through Chaucer and Medieval Drama.* College Outline Series, No. 53. New York, 1961. Page 261.

A very brief discussion. Emphasizes the autobiographical element.

INDEX

Note: nineteenth- and twentieth-century critics and editors are not listed in this index. See footnotes and bibliography.